TEACH
Supernaturally

3 Minute Devotionals That Will Transform Your Teaching!

Tasha N. Askew

ACKNOWLEDGEMENTS

To all of my students who came to teach me just as
much as I came to teach you.

May you rise like the phoenix in front of the sun
and soar as wings on eagles...

I planted the seeds, cultivated, and nourished you.

Now it is your time to thrive! Bloom without apology!
This is your moment!

&

Thank you to my family & friends who have stood patiently by my
side as I've learned to navigate & discover meaning throughout my
tenure as an educator.

DEDICATION

To all my fellow educators who wonder if the rainbow will ever appear in your classroom. Yes it will. Inside of you.

CONTENTS

Week 1

LESSON ONE

WONDER

I f you've taught for any length of time, you will quickly begin to realize that although YOU came to teach your students......THEY most certainly came to teach you too!

I'm reminded of one particular student of mine who had the most intense imagination I'd ever encountered. We'll call him Derek. Initially, it manifested itself as being off task, not paying attention, easily distracted, aloof, and let's just put it out there...hard headed...synonym: stubborn. Ha! That is, until I started delving deeper into my observations of Derek to get to the root of "why" he simply wasn't following my directions.

The most interesting part is my student wasn't intentionally being off task. The more I observed him, the more I realized he couldn't help himself. It was simply a part of whom he was at that age in his life.

Don't get me wrong, I strongly encourage imagination in kids because I believe it's a lost, yet treasured skill. Unfortunately, these days our children have been robbed of their imagination by television, video games, phone apps, and social media. Hence, whenever I meet a student that has somehow managed to hold on to this coveted ability, I quicken to encourage and cultivate this lost art form.

However, this particular school year my students were taking their first standardized test. Dun, dun, duuuunnnn. I know! All eyes are on you, although you're not even the one taking the test! I allowed Derek to explore his imagination daily, creating specific activities just for him, disguised as class lessons so everyone could benefit from exploring this hidden area in their minds and hearts, while also making sure Derek had a creative outlet that would masquerade as opportunities where he wouldn't gain negative behavior points for being off task. I know…sneaky ways to fill a child's bucket.

I decided to start sitting near Derek, just so I could find the gap or missing link in why he couldn't focus during my lessons. The first couple of times he turned his pencil into a dive bomber, I redirected him. After a while, I just sat and watched. I gaped at him setting the scene of an explosion with mere pencils. I observed him turning his crayons into Pokémon characters darting about his desk. I watched him completely check out of the classroom to enter into the land of Jurassic Park with dinosaurs taking over the terrain. All of which wasn't visible to the untrained eye.

I found myself getting lost in Derek's sense of wonder. It was beautiful, albeit not appropriate for the timing of my lessons when the countdown towards test prep blitz had clearly begun. Indeed, Derek's expression of wonder was untimely in my sight, but that year he taught me to never lose my wonder of my Heavenly Father and the plans He has for my life.

As adults we become jaded by our experiences, believing that the bodies we reside in are normal, when that is hardly the case. Our minds have the ability to create images of things that aren't even present. How is that normal? We can hold an image in our minds and interact with it as though we are physically in attendance in that space. Amazing right!?

Today, when you notice one of your students is off task yet again and enamored with pretending their markers are soldiers and their binders are fortresses in the midst of a stately castle, don't be so quick to reprimand them. Take a few moments to relish in their sense of wonder for the world. Reminisce on what it was like when you believed even those things that you couldn't see. Remember what it was like to dream in a space where you didn't have to ask for permission or approval of what your mind created.

May your students revive what it means to wonder and be awed by the phenomenal God you serve. Imagine that He is by your side in every moment as His Word tells you. Envision the Holy Spirit giving you specific directions on how to teach your students today. After all, the Holy Spirit is our help and guidance. May today be a day that your kids remind you to never lose your wonder.

Notes For the Day:

-Matthew 18:3 And he said: Truly I tell you, unless you change and become like little children, you will never enter the kingdom of heaven.

-Romans 15:13 May the God of hope fill you with all joy and peace in believing, so that by the power of the Holy Spirit you may abound in hope.

-Exodus 15:11 Who is like you, O Lord, among the gods? Who is like you, majestic in holiness, awesome in glorious deeds, doing wonders?

Homework:

When was the last time you got caught in "wonder?" Take a minute to mentally go to that place. What do you feel? What thoughts do you have?

_____

_____

_____

_____

_____

_____

_____

_____

_____

_____

_____

_____

_____

_____

_____

_____

_____

_____

_____

LESSON TWO

CALLING

The education profession is not for the faint at heart. I believe we all can agree that this is a profession that no one stumbles in, rather it's a position where individuals are "called" to serve. How many teachers do you know that teach for the sake of simply having a job? Don't misunderstand me. I know some people lose the heart and passion behind why they initially went into the classroom, but I'm pointing out the fact that teaching isn't one of those careers you try on a whim.

John 15:16 says, "You did not choose me, but I chose you and appointed you so that you might go and bear fruit—fruit that will last—and so that whatever you ask in my name the Father will give you." This testifies to the point that you were specifically called to teach at this juncture in your life. Congratulations to you for answering that call! I understand all too well that it isn't an easy one, but I know you've been graced for this!

So what now you say? Serve! Look at each of your students, parents of students, coworkers, and administration and trust that they have all been handpicked to be a part of your life for this time and you theirs. Then begin your purpose! We'll discuss purpose tomorrow. For now, soak in the environment and celebrate that you've taken the first step in obedience.

As scripture reveals, most times, Our Father doesn't assign purpose until the first step has been taken in obedience. You've done just that, so get excited about what is to come! Commit to the mission. There will be days ahead that will tempt you to doubt if you made a sane decision. Moments will beg you to compromise and lose heart in the responsibility you've accepted. Lastly, there will be seasons that call into question your adequacy in fulfilling this role as the leader of handfuls of young minds.

Through it all, you must not waver, but stay strong in the calling that you answered. Romans 8:28 says, "And we know that in all things God works for the good of those who love him, who have been called according to his purpose." This is the Word you confess when you look at your students' test scores and wonder if your hard work means anything. This is the truth you stand on when you have to redirect the same class behavior for the 100th time within the same hour. You are graced to do this work!

Walk in the boldness of knowing that you are not in that classroom by happenstance. You didn't just need a job and fall into a classroom the same day. You were called to this because you have a voice that is capable of speaking into generations. You have an innate ability to cultivate character in children. You are a leader who sets the precedent of leading by serving your kids first and trusting they will follow your example when it is their turn to lead.

Keep your head up and stride in your calling. Take a moment today and recount the time you were "called" into the teaching profession. Allow your story to strengthen you for this work day!

Notes For the Day:

-1 Thessalonians 5:24 The one who calls you is faithful, and He will do it.

-2 Timothy 1:9 He has saved us and called us to a holy life — not because of anything we have done but because of His own purpose and grace. This grace was given us in Christ Jesus before the beginning of time,

-1 Peter 1:15-16 But just as He who called you is holy, so be holy in all you do; for it is written: "Be holy, because I am holy."

Homework:

Write the words "Why I Teach" in the center of a sheet of paper. In the remaining white space right down phrases that answer this question for you. Hang this sheet on the wall behind your teacher desk so you can reflect each morning.

_____

_____

_____

_____

_____

_____

_____

LESSON THREE

PURPOSE

Ephesians 2:10 says, "For we are God's masterpiece. He has created us anew in Christ Jesus, so we can do the good things he planned for us long ago." Everything changed the day the scales were removed from my eyes concerning my true purpose as a teacher. Nope. My purpose as a teacher was not revealed on my teaching contract underneath the job description. No, it was not revealed to me by my principal. Furthermore, it was not revealed to me through the mandates of the school district and their expectations of me as prescribed by the state department of education. My purpose as an educator was revealed to me by Our Heavenly Father.

It was the crispy and refreshing fall season. My students had just taken their first benchmarks of the school year, and we all were headed to the freedom better known as fall break. The benchmark scores were in, and I thought I'd take a glance at them before heading out to enjoy my sweet days of solitude, joy, and rest that were before me. Wrong idea! Instead, all I did was open a can of worms.

As I sat behind my desk pouring the weight of my head into my cupped hands, defeat started to parade around my classroom. I looked at the data of the students I'd been working the hardest with, only to find out that they were still at the bottom of the academic totem pole. Ugghh... My once joyous smile leveled out to be parallel with my desk and all I could do was sulk in the disappointment that I'd spent my afternoons and nights, and don't forget the times I compromised not being with family on the weekends, just to see to it that my students were successful. Was this the evidence I deserved!?? It paled so harshly with my reality.

I paced the classroom slowly for some time in silence allowing my thoughts to run their damaging course on my spirit. The building appeared to be asleep, due to the fact that everyone else was out enjoying fall football games, sweater weather, warm drinks, and breaking in their fashionable boots and scarfs. I felt as hopeless as Chuck on the episode of Charlie Brown when Snoopy hadn't come home. I gathered my teacher bag, glimpsed dismally at the classroom, flipped the light switch and sauntered out of the building.

It wasn't long before Our Father started speaking to me. He wasn't about to let His daughter start her vacation on that note. He's such a good Father. During that drive home He asked me, "Daughter, did you teach them to the best of your ability?" I eagerly replied, "Yes, I did. I did the best I knew how to do." He said, "Did you give them your all?" I belted out, "Abba you know I did that and then some. I sacrificed time with my family for them!"

At this point the tears were streaming down my face like a tub that'd been unplugged. He inquired, "What is your mission in that classroom?" I replied, " My mission is to love them, develop them, and teach them so that they will be strong servant leaders for their generation impacting and changing this world for the better." Then He whispered, "So why are you disappointed if you know that's what you've been doing?" I blurted, "......because they want me to get 100% of the students to pass every test every time and I didn't do that! I have to prove that I can do that Daddy!"

At that moment, He stopped me and presented me with one of the most profound lessons I've ever received. He began,

"Daughter, I called and placed you in that classroom. Don't think for one moment that your principal, the hiring committee, or even you placed yourself in that position. I placed you there for My glory. I always knew in this season you'd be a teacher because I planned it. I strategically handpicked the students in your class for a reason. There are certain gifts, abilities, and seeds I've placed in you because I knew I could count on you to sow them properly in the right students. Those kids need what I placed in you over 2,000 years ago. I orchestrated for them to receive certain things from you and you only. The coworkers that are in your path and the parents of your students are all in your life on purpose. There are precise conversations that I've arranged, traits I've planned to develop in you, and happenings I've purposed to manifest during this time. I placed you in that classroom in order that you would follow My mission for you, not the school district's mission or your principals, or the state department of education. Yes, you need to be respectful to your Earthly authority, but since when do the words of man trump the words of your God? When do your Lord's desires take a backseat to the world's plans? When did the King of all Kings, Alpha and Omega, your loving Abba Father become replaced by the opinions and expectations of society? Never. Now you go out and enjoy every moment of this vacation. You are my daughter who I approve of always. Do the best you know how in teaching and preparing your students, but don't sacrifice this abundant life I've called you to live. Enjoy Me, your family, friends, yourself, and your life. You are on the perfect path I laid out just for you!"

Notes For the Day:

-Philippians 2:13 For God is working in you, giving you the desire and the power to do what pleases him.

-John 10:10 The thief's purpose is to steal and kill and destroy. My purpose is to give them a rich and satisfying life.

-Galatians 1:10 For am I now seeking the approval of man, or of God? Or am I trying to please man? If I were still trying to please man, I would not be a servant of Christ.

Homework:

Take 30 minutes out of your day to journal to your Heavenly Father and ask Him what is the purpose for which He has called you to the classroom.

_____

_____

_____

_____

_____

_____

_____

_____

_____

_____

LESSON FOUR

COURAGE

I remember it just like it was yesterday. I'd left my position at CNN in Atlanta and was headed for a nine-hour drive back home. The world was my canvas, and I'd yet to find out what mesmerizing art lay within me. The economy had taken a fall for the worst, and in the meantime, a friend suggested I try my hand at substitute teaching. "Oh noooo!" was my reply. "I didn't go to college to earn a bachelor's degree in a completely different field just to throw it away on substitute teaching. No thank you!"

My friend responded curiously, "What do you have to lose? Just do it to earn some money while you look for the career you really want." Pride raised its ugly head and told me no, but the still small Voice said, "Go for it."

It took courage for me to sulk away from the degree training and professional experiences I'd accumulated over the past 5 years and walk blindly into the classroom, but oh was it exhilarating! I stepped into a world that I only remembered fondly as a child.

As a little girl, I had such a voracious appetite for learning. I would corral my sister into "playing school" with our dolls and stuffed animals, and I would even tote a math book over to a receptive adult, asking them to teach me what was in the book, although I was all of four years old. I know. I was an intense child. Ha!

As I navigated the world of substitute teaching, I discovered that I was a voice for those who couldn't speak loud enough for themselves: children. I found the sweet spot that lay dormant within me that began to resound advocacy for kids who didn't speak English and even those who were labeled with a mental or physical impediment.

Fast forward the time, and I found myself boldly answering a call that was BIGGER than I. You know, the call that you receive from your super supportive Heavenly Father when you'd rather practice displaying slight amnesia. He poured into my spirit, "Love them, lead them, and then teach them." I could no longer see kids as "kids" but rather I began to see them as dynamic leaders that I would cultivate into "lights" that would dispel world darkness.

Ambitious right, but why not? Why not change the world one child at a time? Why not do the best you know how with what you have been given? Why not be bold enough to not just teach them, but start with the foundation of loving, leading, and serving them in expectation that they will follow your lead, and reverberate what they've learned from you in all of 10 months to the entire world? Why not? Why not advocate for them in a way that supports their spirit and not simply their standardized test scores?

One word: COURAGE.

If you are teaching a class, believe that Our Heavenly Father has graced you with the courage that is able to fortify an ant to lift a brick house. Yes, it's that deep! There is such power in the small things! Don't despise your humble beginnings. Yes, you are "just" a classroom teacher, but YES YOU ARE A CLASSROOM TEACHER!

You have been given the charge to step into courage, walk in it with your head up, and show up for your kids even on the days you question how and why you chose to teach in the first place. Trust me, I've been there plenty of times. Yes, it gets tough, and I'd be lying to you if I said the useless meetings were going to come to an end, the pressure for you to dictate your students' performance on standardized tests was over, or that it would be understood that you of all people actually do need help, support, and encouragement to continue with a smile in front of your students every day. Go figure!

Yet it's so worth it and for this appointed time, you have been given the charge to show up courageous for them. They depend on you! Exchange your frustration, disappointment, exhaustion, and anger with Your Father for His peace. Believe it! You are COURAGEOUS!

Notes For the Day:

- Isaiah 41:10 So do not fear for I am with you; do not be dismayed, for I am your God. I will strengthen you and help you; I will uphold you with my righteous right hand.

- Hebrews 13:5-6 For He Himself has said, "I will never leave you nor forsake you." So we may boldly say: "The LORD is my helper; I will not fear. What can man do to me?"

- 1 Chronicles 28:20 David also said to Solomon his son, "Be strong and courageous, and do the work. Do not be afraid or discouraged, for the LORD God, my God, is with you. He will not fail you or forsake you until all the work for the service of the temple of the LORD is finished.

Homework:

List one opportunity where you can show up courageous for your kids today.

_____

_____

_____

_____

_____

_____

_____

_____

_____

_____

_____

_____

_____

_____

_____

_____

_____

_____

LESSON FIVE

GRACE

It was a normal school day. My students and I were in the midst of a lesson. I'd called on one of my scholars randomly after observing her being off task. I didn't intend for it to serve as a "gotcha" moment, but to bring awareness to the fact that she was off task and redirect her so she wouldn't continue to miss the meat of the lesson.

"So....who can remind me of the definition of a character trait?" I announced in a jolly voice. I peered around the classroom for a moment at all of the eager hands flailing about, and then I zeroed in on my child who was completely zoned out. BINGO! "Stacy? Remind us of the definition of a character trait." Stacy looked up from the distracting markers and stickers she'd somehow allowed to grace our reading lesson. It seemed as though her eyes grew the size of jawbreakers! She had no clue how to answer me.

I gave her a bit of wait time, being the great teacher that I am, and seeing as though children take quite a bit of time to process and then carefully form their words to articulate a response. My point wasn't to embarrass her, but to show her the pattern of what happens when you are off task. Simply put, I was training her to be alert and engaged.

Several seconds later, I moved on to phrase the question to another child. "Brandon, can you help Stacy remember the definition of a character trait?" Brandon answered with ease. I quickly shot a knowing glance back at Stacy to hint to her that she wasn't off the hook, and I'd be back to review that same question with her. She withdrew her sigh of relief.

I allowed some time to pass during the lesson, in an effort to give Stacy the opportunity to marinate in the definition. It was time! I glanced about the class and posed the question yet again. "Ok, so remind me once more what we said was the definition of a character trait." This time I knew for sure that Stacy would get it right. After all, we did exchange a conversation via our eyes and that always works right?

Wrong. Stacy was zero and two. Somehow, now there was a glitter pen that ambushed her imagination! Sheesh! I repeated the same process above and said a silent prayer that this time Stacy would be alert to my teaching pattern and class expectation. I shot my glance her way and tilted my head a bit so as to say, "Young lady, I'm coming back for you and this time that definition needs to roll off your tongue as smooth as butter."

The clock had struck! It was time! With my fingers crossed, I proceeded to phrase the question for the last time. By the way, this repetition is excellent for your other students who struggle to retain information. This time I waited a little longer for Stacy's response, all the while cheering her on in my mind. "You got this girl! Don't fail me now! Stacy, I don't want to make an example out of you! Just say the definition we rehearsed!"

Within a few moments Stacy's lips were positioned, and before I knew it the definition came falling down like sweet rain after a drought! The class went wild! (Yes, I'm that teacher who makes a celebration out of everything, and it's incredibly contagious with my students.) We celebrated Stacy's victory, and she smiled so big I could even see her molars! Boy was she proud!

That day, I was reminded of the grace of Our Heavenly Father. How many times have you thought that you missed an opportunity for a blessing that our Father presented to you? Have you ever regretted a time when you didn't act or speak in accordance with what Our Father told you? Trust me. You're not alone. I've been there, beating myself up for not being able to rewrite my personal history book. However, Our Father taught me a lesson through Stacy that day. His grace is sufficient.

He is the God of second and even third chances. I cared for Stacy and loved her so much that I wanted to see her be successful. As such, I set it up purposely, so she would be triumphant. I could have stopped at her one incorrect answer and scolded her for not being on task. I could have even embarrassed her the second time she missed the mark, but that wasn't the point. The point was that she began to understand her pattern as well as my expectations. She needed to understand that she was in a safe space to grow into the fullness of whom she was designed to be. She needed affirmation that it is ok to "fail" as long as you learn from it and persevere. She needed the comfort of knowing that I was for her and not against her just as Our Father is for us. She needed to know that I would provide her with opportunities to change her narrative as long as she was postured to truly make an effort, just as Our Father wants us to know His grace is sufficient as we keep our hearts pure before Him.

Don't beat yourself up anymore if you are ashamed of an opportunity that you believe you missed. Take heart in the truth that Our Father is faithful, and He wants to see you win! He delights in seeing you prosper! He knows that you are not perfect in your own strength and that you fall short. In spite of all of that, He still wants to be there to cheer you on to your victory just like all of my students and I did for Stacy when she answered correctly. All of heaven and His angel armies are shouting and clapping loudly for your victory! Standing ovation!

Notes For the Day:

-2 Corinthian 12:9 But he said to me, "My grace is sufficient for you, for my power is made perfect in weakness." Therefore I will boast all the more gladly about my weaknesses, so that Christ's power may rest on me.

-Psalm 35:27 May those who delight in my vindication shout for joy and gladness; may they always say, "The LORD be exalted, who delights in the well-being of his servant."

-Luke 15:7 "I tell you that in the same way, there will be more joy in heaven over one sinner who repents than over ninety-nine righteous persons who need no repentance."

Homework:

Meditate on 2 Corinthian 12:9. To what specific event in your life do you need to apply this scripture?

_____

_____

_____

_____

_____

Week 2

LESSON SIX

STEWARDSHIP

Too often as a teacher, I had the opportunity to bypass and ignore things I saw students doing in the building. You know the things that kids do when they know it's clearly wrong, yet they do it just to see how far they can get away with it? Let me jog your memory. Visualize students running down the halls, yelling in the restrooms, chasing other students, using inappropriate language, and the list goes on. Certainly, that wasn't just the case for the school campuses I've worked on? Ha! At any rate, those are the moments I'm referencing.

I cannot recall the number of times I could have pretended to not notice a situation that needed to be addressed by an adult. If you haven't drawn the conclusion yet, yes, I was raised with the "village" mentality. It takes a village to raise a child. Essentially, what that means is it is permissible by unspoken waiver for any loving and healthy adult that happens to be in a child's presence at the moment of much-needed correction, to do so accordingly. As life would happen, I also took that frame of mind into my teaching career. Let me set the stage for you.

The dismissal bell had rung about 30 minutes prior, and I was heading back to my classroom to prepare for the following day. I know. I should have had my bag and keys in tow and skipped to my car as soon as my last kid fist-bumped me at the sight of his parent. Let's be truthful. There's a hardcore group of us who just have to go back into the classroom to try to improve something for the one billionth time!

Before I continue, let me give you a bit more context. At the time, I was the only African American teacher, teaching at a predominately Hispanic elementary-middle school duo. Yes, out of approximately one hundred faculty and staff members I was the only one with ginger toffee complected skin and there was a small handful (enough to count on one hand) of children with whom I shared a common ethnic background. Now that wasn't a problem for me at all. I've always adapted to culture well. However, this day was a little different.

I was strutting down the hallway in my heels. Yup, I was that teacher. If you're going to teach, you might as well look good doing it! I hadn't made it to the last corridor before I heard a young man's voice yell a string of words, in which the only word that made contact with my cerebral was the... racial slur! I froze in my tracks! I thought, "There is no way in the world that word came out of the body of one of these middle school students!" I turned around to see a throng of children in the hallway, apparently headed to afterschool tutoring.

At that moment, the "village mentality" consumed me. I announced loud and clear in a stern, yet adamant manner that caused the entire hallway scene to freeze like icicles on a brutally cold day in Wisconsin winter, "Who just said that word!?" I glared around at the faces that were now confirming in their minds that they knew staying afterschool for tutoring wasn't a good idea.

"Did you say it?" I interrogated the young man directly behind me. "No ma'am. He said it," pointing to the young man who'd just retreated into a nearby classroom. I immediately barged my way into those four walls to get permission to speak with this student, who for a moment thought to show annoyance of me actually locating him. He was an 8th grader. In less than two seconds, the temperaments of four generations of intense women in my family beckoned! I quickly reprimanded the student and showed him what respect looked like as I led him into the corridor.

As he retold the story of what he said in the hallway, detailing how he was calling "another student" that "racial slur" (who by the way, was not of African American descent,) simply because that is what they call each other. "We don't say it to be mean. It's just like we're saying homie." I discerned that the young man, we'll call him Joseph, was actually sincere. As my anger and passion began to deflate, I asked him if he knew the history of that word and the demographic it impacts. He replied with an uneasy, "No." That day Joseph learned one of the toughest lessons he'll probably ever learn in life.

Needless to say, Joseph and I began to develop an understanding and healthy respect for one another. From that day forth, I directed him to report to me on the history of such terminology, and I forced him to enlarge his capacity for compassion, social justice and dignity until he went off to high school. Every time I would see Joseph in the hallway, he addressed me as ma'am and used other polite salutations with me. I noticed his entire demeanor changed when he was around other students. It was almost as if he was a lion poking his chest out. You could tell he was proud of his evolution in just a few short weeks. He gained a jewel that he realized none of his peers possessed.

Not only did I teach Joseph a lesson in the hallway that day, but I also spoke life into his identity. I gave vision to the man he was that he didn't even know existed. I spoke to the leader in him that hadn't been discovered yet. I spoke to the man in him who would cause others to shift and recognize the inherent power of words.

Understand that Our Father has set you in that classroom on assignment. You've been placed in your very school environment on a mission. Your mission is to steward well the kids that have been entrusted to you. It is your responsibility to gift the children in your school with the gifts that are within you, and yes that may come in the form of sharing cultural wisdom. When I saw Joseph, I didn't see an 8th grader gone rogue. I saw a man who would one day play a major role in the social order. To that end, he would either contribute to the injustice and cruelty that constantly revolves in society, or he would be shifting the dialogue of humanity to one that honors uniqueness and fosters equality. I realized that I'd been given the opportunity to influence the trajectory of his future, by taking a few moments to recognize the position Our Father had given me and steward it well.

The next time you're thinking about walking past that wayward child, stop and lean in. Ask the Holy Spirit how He wants you to steward that moment, and if He needs you to step into a child's life to alter the trajectory of the future. Be bold!

Notes For the Day:

-Luke 12:48 From everyone who has been given much, much will be demanded; and from the one who has been entrusted with much, much more will be asked.

-Colossians 3:23-24 Whatever you do, do it enthusiastically, as something done for the Lord and not for men, knowing that you will receive the reward of an inheritance from the Lord. You serve the Lord Christ.

– 1 Peter 4:10 Based on the gift each one has received, use it to serve others, as good managers of the varied grace of God.

Homework:

What has Our Father asked you to steward this school year?

_____

_____

_____

_____

_____

_____

_____

LESSON SEVEN

HOPE

As though you don't already have enough on your plate as a teacher, there's one more hat I need to add to your collection: hope dealer. One of the main components of being a teacher is that you are a beacon of what is possible for your students as well as the surrounding adults. Hope is a foreign concept these days. In this context, we'll define hope as an expectation of good.

Unbeknownst to those who don't work in the school system, a school is a prime location for disappointment, frustration, anger, agitation, and weariness to unfold. Most people are blinded by the colorful displays of student work that scream joy, or the vibrant chatter of voices and laughter that pour out of classrooms. Deep within those walls, teachers understand the potential of a very different reality plagued with cynicism and apathy if one is not careful. Why subject yourself to that force when you are in charge of the narrative?

As you begin your day, you are responsible for setting your affections on those things you desire. The things you focus on are the things you welcome into your world. You determine your responses to less than favorable conditions. I cannot tell you the number of times I forced myself to choose joy when an RTI meeting was rescheduled or when a student vomited in class and "interrupted" the flow of the lesson. How about when a fine arts teacher failed to receive my students for class or how I simply forgot to run the copies for the reading assessment one week. Sheesh! I think I have a nerve that twitches whenever I have to make copies.

The bottom line is, you must choose to be a bearer of light. In Matthew 5:14 Jesus said, "You are the light of the world. A city set on a hill cannot be hidden." So let your light shine for all to see! Smile. Speak words that give birth to life. He continued in the next verse by saying, "Neither do people light a lamp and put it under a bowl. Instead, they put it on its stand, and it gives light to everyone in the house." The glory that has been placed in you shall not go to waste! Share it with your coworkers, administration, parents of your students, and your students!

You'll always have an opportunity to choose the low road, but oh what a difference it makes when you set your intention on vibrating higher each day. Early in the morning, command your day and tell it how to unfold. I did that each morning before I would let my students in the classroom. I would pray over my class environment asking Him to blanket the room in peace as well as ensure smooth dispersal of information like the dew on the morning grass. I would speak over my students, especially those with behavior challenges to come in alignment with decency and order as He declared in 1 Corinthians 14:40. I would conclude in surrender for Him to take over my tongue and disposition as I yield to Him so His essence could cascade from me and lay beautifully upon all I encountered that day. Most importantly, I would thank Him for choosing me as His vessel to speak into the generations of humans that would go on to shift the culture and climate of the world.

You too have this ability. Just do it! Don't let anyone steal your hope. Let me remind you of Hebrews 6:19 that says, "We have this hope as an anchor for the soul, firm and secure. It enters the inner sanctuary behind the curtain.." Anchors are meant to connect to a body of water (The Word of God) to prevent the vessel (You) from drifting due to the winds or currents (circumstances and events that occur). Be of good hope and cheer today!

Notes For the Day:

-Romans 15:13 May the God of hope fill you with all joy and peace as you trust in him, so that you may overflow with hope by the power of the Holy Spirit.

-Psalm 147:11 the LORD delights in those who fear him, who put their hope in his unfailing love.

-Matthew 5:16 In the same way, let your light shine before others, that they may see your good deeds and glorify your Father in heaven.

Homework:

Colossians 3:2 says, "Set your affection on things above, not on things on the earth." What things do you need to set your affections on today?

_____

_____

_____

_____

LESSON EIGHT

PATIENCE

I'll never forget the day that Our Heavenly Father showed me the parallel between myself and one of my students serving as a translation of myself and Him. Get ready. This one's a doozy.

First, let me give you a bit of context. It was Back To School Night, and as always, I was aiming to build relationships with my students' parents before I met their child on the first day of school. When I met Justin's mother for the first time, she pulled me to the side to divulge, "I just want to apologize in advance. My son has a bit of an anger issue. I'm sorry. If you have, any questions please call me." Yup, just like that. No hello, how are you doing? Just the immediate word vomit of an apology about her son in whom I'd yet to meet.

I replied in the most sincere, yet "let me make one thing clear" manner. "Ohhh….ma'am, just so you know, I am a very fun teacher. Yet, I am a "no nonsense" type of teacher." (Did you hear my voice change on the latter sentence?) "Children do not have anger problems. He will adjust to me very quickly, and he'll be just fine." With that, I smiled and moved on to the next parent.

The next day I was warned by a few other teachers of the terrors that this student caused in previous years. Don't get me wrong, I was dumbfounded at the stories they shared with me regarding Justin, but neither my spirit nor mind was phased.

You see, I had quite the reputation at my school as the super fun teacher, but the incredibly strict disciplinarian. The kids would beg to be in my class, but they knew behaviorally, they needed to be on their p's and q's. It was somewhat of an unspoken rule. Make sure you NEVER have to go to Ms. Askew for discipline issues but try your best to get into her class because she's so much fun! Needless to say, I ended up having Justin for 3 years at the request of his parents.

Enough context. Let me get to the meat of the story. We were in the middle of a lesson and all of a sudden I noticed some of the kids' gazes shooting nervously back to Justin. I immediately knew we were probably headed to a family meeting. That is, a "class family meeting" if you know what I mean. Justin was about to have what I liked to refer to as "a moment." "A moment" simply meant a time where he would revert to his old self with "anger issues" before he met me. I pretended not to notice in an effort to give Justin an opportunity to resolve his inner conflict. As I walked around the room pretending to be extremely interested in each students' work, I kept my eyes on Justin to see how the scenario would play out.

Justin's face begin to turn cherry tomato, red and his facial expression began to tighten. All the while, I pretended not to notice. Then came the physical harm. I saw him grab his arm in an attempt to scratch it like a lion clawing at freshly captured prey. I immediately shot a stare in his direction and announced his name piercingly. He looked up like a deer caught in headlights because he knew the thousands of conversations we'd had regarding solving inner conflict. (Picture that. Eight-year olds learning to resolve inner conflict. Imagine the condition of the world if all children learned this.)

Back to the story. I proceeded to slowly, yet sternly as only a mother could to her child, speak to him with the aim of strategically facilitating his own dialogue that would bring him back to his center. I must admit. I was quite upset myself because I just couldn't fathom how he could arrive at this place of being mentally out of control after we'd had this conversation innumerable times.

I began calmly, "Justin, the first time you lose your temper, it's an accident and then you learn from it. All of the times after that it's intentional. Why in the world do you keep doing the same thing if you already know the end result? We've discussed patterns, and you know yours all too well. With that being said, tell me why?" He proceeded to tell me the effects. "So why do you repeat the same undesirable actions so many times!?" I countered, a bit annoyed. Can you tell my kids became vocabulary masters after spending a year with me?

That is when I knew it was time for me to be quiet and show him the greatest amount of grace I knew to give. Justin went on to tell me how he'd been telling his brain to stay calm and to complete his work. He said he kept talking to himself about the right steps to take, but somehow he lost it. He broke down in tears while staring at the look of disappointment on my face. He said, " Every time I try to do the right thing, I always do the opposite! EVERY SINGLE TIME, AND I DON'T KNOW WHY!"

In that moment, the Holy Spirit whispered softly to me, "Doesn't this remind you of yourself daughter? How many times have you wanted to think differently about something, be more generous, tame your tongue, lose weight, start a new venture, discipline yourself in an area and every time the opportunity arises you don't show up as the ideal version of yourself?" Ahhhhhhhh!!! I was convicted. He said,

"Daughter, what is my response to you in those moments? Do I still love you into your development? Do I get angry at you and cast you away? Am I patient with you even though I've told you the same thing a million times over? Do I still extend my grace and encouragement to you?"

You might as well had handed both Justin and I a tissue because in that moment this scripture came to me: Romans 7:15-20:

> *"I do not understand what I do. For what I want to do I do not do, but what I hate I do. And if I do what I do not want to do, I agree that the law is good. As it is, it is no longer I myself who do it, but it is sin living in me. For I know that good itself does not dwell in me, that is, in my sinful nature. For I have the desire to do what is good, but I cannot carry it out. For I do not do the good I want to do, but the evil I do not want to do – this I keep on doing. Now if I do what I do not want to do, it is no longer I who do it, but it is sin living in me that does it."*

All I could hear was...patience... patience...patience. It echoed in my ears like a lost child shouting for its mother in the Grand Canyon. Just as Our loving Father extends endless patience with us each day, we have to show up for our kids in the same way. There isn't any difference in OUR inability and struggle to transform than in a child's beside their age. When your challenging student has "a moment" today, remember how Your Heavenly Father deals with you when you are trying, yet you still seem to come up short. Give them the gift of your patience. Patience will transform them in ways you couldn't even imagine.

Notes For the Day:

-Habakkuk 2:3 *For the revelation awaits an appointed time; it speaks of the end and will not prove false. Though it linger, wait for it; it will certainly come and will not delay.*

-Proverbs 15:18 *Hot tempers cause arguments, but patience brings peace.*

-1 Corinthian 13:4 *Love is patient and kind; it is not jealous or conceited or proud.*

Homework:

Patience is a skill. When you are presented with an opportunity to exercise patience, what should you do first to get you started down this more gentle path?

_____

_____

_____

_____

_____

_____

_____

_____

_____

_____

_____

_____

_____

_____

_____

_____

_____

_____

LESSON NINE

PERSEVERANCE

I nicknamed Ranada the "Poster Child for Perseverance." Yup, I even shared this moniker with her parents and our entire class family. Honestly speaking, I was in awe of Ranada's tenacity. Ranada was a student who was considered Tier 3, the lowest on the academic educational ranking. In order to be successful she would require quite a bit of intervention. Was there anything wrong with that? Not at all. It was just the reality of where she stood academically and the effort that needed to be put in from all stakeholders in order to shore up her strengths.

Here's the beautiful surprise about Ranada's situation. Behaviorally speaking, she was excellent! I know right? How much easier is it to help a student make progress when their behavior is a non-issue? Ranada was one of those students who simply needed more than the average amount of time to process material. She paid attention in class, completed her assignments to the best of her ability, returned her homework daily, and she even participated in the lessons! Still, she scored incredibly low on tests and quizzes. These are the phenomenon that allude to teacher insomnia.

Ranada attended every single tutoring session I held that school year. My goodness did I hold a lot of them. She even attended intercession school, which were intervention classes for students over fall and spring breaks. There were times I even felt sorry for her because I could see that she was trying very hard, but it just wasn't making a difference, or so it appeared.

I used Ranada's actions and attitude many times during class lessons to exemplify the meaning of perseverance to the rest of my students. We championed Ranada for her steadfastness. I gave them the analogy that kids are like plants to give them a better understanding of what was happening with Ranada.

I described how when we want a plant, we get a seed first. We deposit the seed into the soil. Day after day, we water the seed, place it in the sunlight, and nourish it the best we know how in order to support its growth. We can't yell at the seed to make it grow. We can't even give it a deadline to grow. We can't snap our fingers and command it to grow at the sound of our voice. However, when it is the seed's appointed time to grow, it will. It will bloom and flourish beyond anything we could have anticipated.

I told Ranada she was just like that seed, and when it was her time, it would happen and no one would be able to stop her. I encouraged her not to focus solely on her test scores, but to imagine the scores she wanted to see on her papers. I was teaching her to activate her eyes of faith, without using those exact words. Throughout the year, I continued to praise her and remind her that her time was coming soon. In my mind, I knew even if her moment didn't come that school year, it would still come right on time.

Fast forward to the second week of summer break and I received a text from Ranada's mom. She said she'd received Ranada's state standardized test scores! She passed both of them by the skin of her teeth!! I was ecstatic!! I told her to give Ranada a huge hug for me, tell her I said you go girl, and let her know that her time to bloom had come! I knew Ranada would know exactly what I meant. Her mom revealed that Ranada smiled so big she thought her face was hurting. I could just see her sparkling braces and beautiful brown eyes light up now.

Ranada confirmed for me the power in never giving up. She reminded me of simple truths Our Father teaches us in that we are responsible for sowing, but truly He is the author of the harvest. Keep pushing. What looks like nothing is just the seed preparing to burst through the surface!

Notes For the Day:

-Galatians 6:9 Let us not become weary in doing good, for at the proper time we will reap a harvest if we do not give up.

-James 1:12 Blessed is the one who perseveres under trial because, having stood the test, that person will receive the crown of life that the Lord has promised to those who love him.

-Ecclesiastes 9:11 I have seen something else under the sun: The race is not to the swift or the battle to the strong, nor does food come to the wise or wealth to the brilliant or favor to the learned; but time and chance happen to them all.

Homework:

Which one of your students do you need to praise and encourage to keep putting one foot in front of the other each day? Where do you need to continue persevering in your life?

_____

_____

_____

_____

_____

_____

LESSON TEN

REST

Rest. Is that even a word in a teacher's vocabulary? Well, if it hasn't been an intentional word that cascades beautifully from your mouth, it needs to be. Our Father set the example during the week of Creation to exemplify the necessity of resting after you've done your best. It is fundamental in order to function as a co-partner in creating. He put it this way in Genesis 2:2, "By the seventh day God had finished the work He had been doing; so on the seventh day he rested from all his work."

Notice it doesn't say He rested because He was tired. Instead, He rested because He was finished, and He saw that His work was good. Yup, you guessed it! Here comes my story.

Throughout my years of teaching, standardized tests were all the rave. One would bring to question if school was indeed a safe space for a child to develop into the fullness of their expression, or if it was simply a place to practice rote memorization.

Nevertheless, there were always opportunities to sacrifice spring, summer, and fall breaks to continue grinding at the mill. This is not an exhortation to not participate in any additional reinforcements for your students. I recommend that you seek Our Father in prayer and allow Him to give you specifics on how He wants you to sow, lead, and manage your scholars. Yet for me, because I gave 500% daily with my students, I never felt convicted to participate in any of the "intervention sessions" that happened to take place during my vacation periods.

I knew I'd given EVERYTHING I had to my students. I'd poured into them as best as I knew how. I'd labored over changing lesson plans a plethora of times, just to accommodate the fluctuations in my students' learning. Although my kids may not have been precisely where I wanted them to be academically at any given moment, I knew rest was summoning my soul.

Our responsibility as teachers is to sow in the best way we know how using acquired knowledge and skills and then release our students to Our Father to be in charge of the harvest. Growth is not anymore your job than it is a farmer's who just planted a crop. Yes, you must nourish and support a child, but never forget there is no amount of effort that you can do that will possibly cause the child to "actually" grow. Think about it, yelling at a corn crop or repeating the same words over and over to a crop will not cause it to germinate any sooner than the appointed time.

After you have put forth your best effort, and I truly mean you have given your all as is possible to maintain your sanity, let it go and rest. You need to recharge and you deserve it! There is no way that you will function optimally if you are running on empty. An empty pot cannot pour, so just calm down, advocate for your peace, and then rest. Let me be the first to say, "You are doing a PHENOMENAL JOB!! You are rocking it! Even though you may feel like you are sinking into a dark abyss, you aren't! Even termites can't tell they are about to destroy a mansion with their little one-fourth of inch bodies! It's the small things in life that amount to the large transformations. Take a day or more and just rest.

Notes For the Day:

-Matthew 11:28-30 Come to me, all you who are weary and burdened, and I will give you rest. Take my yoke upon you and learn from me, for I am gentle and humble in heart, and you will find rest for your souls. For my yoke is easy and my burden is light.

-Hebrews 4: 9-11 Let us therefore strive to enter that rest, so that no one may fall by the same sort of disobedience.

-Psalm 127:1-2 Unless the Lord builds the house, those who build it labor in vain. Unless the Lord guards the city, the guard keeps watch in vain. It is in vain that you rise up early and go late to rest, eating the bread of anxious toil; for he gives sleep to his beloved.

Homework:

What can you do today to rest after work? Do you need to take off for a mental health day from work?

_____

_____

_____

_____

_____

Week 3

LESSON ELEVEN

GENTLENESS

As an educator, it's easy to fall into the pressure trap of being hard on yourself. You can run down your laundry list of items you have yet to do, think about areas wherein you didn't do enough, and even cringe at the areas in which you "appeared" unsuccessful. In spite of it all, the one thing we need to remember is to be gentle with ourselves.

I strongly suggest as a teacher that you plan several "mental health" days throughout the school year. My first two years in the classroom, I didn't take off a single day because I wanted to be the savior of mankind in my classroom. I didn't want to disappoint my administration. I wanted to be there for my kids. I wanted to prove myself to whom and for what I still can't quite conclude. However, as my tenure in the classroom progressed, I quickly learned if I wasn't gentle with myself, I was bound to crumble in front of my students.

As human beings, we have an innate receptiveness for tender touches and mellow sounds. Did you know that gentleness is one of the fruits of the Spirit? We are predisposed to exemplify gentleness as children of the Most High. It's this very tenderness that enables us to evolve well. Think about it. When you explain a concept to a student who is already confused and frustrated, do they receive it better when you are yelling at them or when you are taking your time while using a calm voice?

Our bodies are the same way. When you condemn yourself for being an awful teacher, how do you anticipate being able to perform optimally or even take on more responsibility than what you're currently managing? Slow down and be kind to yourself. Take a few deep breaths. Repeat aloud that you are doing a phenomenal job. Ask yourself what you need in this moment to be ok? Turn on some worship music or nature sounds during your planning period and just relax on your carpet until it's time to retrieve your students. Bring your favorite hand moisturizer to work and massage your hands for 5 minutes before the morning bell rings. Go get a massage after school.

Whatever you do, remember your temple (your body) does a lot for you. Take a moment to appreciate your Creator for the wonderous creation that He designed you as, and do it gently. Everything is and will be ok.

Notes For the Day:

-Galatians 5:22-23 But the fruit of the Spirit is love, joy, peace, forbearance, kindness, goodness, faithfulness, gentleness and self-control. Against such things there is no law.

-Matthew 11:29 Take My yoke upon you and learn from Me, for I am gentle and humble in heart, and YOU WILL FIND REST FOR YOUR SOULS.

-Matthew 5:5 Blessed are the gentle, for they shall inherit the earth.

Homework:

Pause throughout the day and confess this scripture aloud until you feel yourself changing from within.

"I pursue righteousness, godliness, faith, love, perseverance and gentleness." 1 Timothy 6:11

_____

_____

_____

_____

_____

_____

_____

_____

_____

_____

_____

_____

_____

_____

LESSON TWELVE

PEACE

Peace as juxtaposed to chaos was something I intentionally taught my students. From the onset of the year, my students were engaged in interactive exercises to understand what constituted peace versus what could be identified as chaos.

In the majority of cases, children are at a disadvantage when it comes to verbalizing emotional states and processing internal and external stimuli. In other words, you have to feed them instructions on how to navigate their environments and process their feelings. This takes a premeditated stance from the educator's perspective.

It was the spring of the school year, and I'd called a "family meeting" because I began to see a pattern of my students not completing their classwork while in Daily 5 stations. For those who are unfamiliar,

Daily 5 stations is basically a time where the teacher works with a small group of children for intervention, while the rest of the class is divvied into small groups to work on specific tasks. Review skills constitute the work completed by the students who are not assigned to the teacher's small group. That way, students don't need assistance with their assignments.

Yet this day, as I was working with my small group, I noticed that the other students in the class did not appear to actually be getting any work done. You know how it goes. One student is day dreaming in the corner, another is playing with scissors, two others are holding a deep conversation about the birthday party they are having this weekend, while yet another is upside down on the floor turning a bottle of glue into a super hero. Father help my unbelief. Ha!

Typically during Daily 5 a teacher will not stop to correct behavior because you'll never accomplish what you need to get done with your small group. This day, I knew we were in for an intense "family meeting" when Daily 5 was over. In spite of the frustration threatening to surface and spill out of my mouth, I remained calm and pretended everything was per usual. Then I called the meeting. The expressions on my students' faces were worthy of a Kodak! They had no clue what went wrong, but you could tell they were fishing for what they "could have" done incorrectly with it only being 3 hours into the school day.

As I facilitated the discussion, which I was accustomed to doing at this point since they'd started getting better at leading conflict resolution in these meetings, I heard the word peaceful. One of my students had already fast forwarded to the resolution stage and was announcing what needed to happen during Daily 5 tomorrow. Kendrik stood proudly and said, "Today was a little chaotic because everyone was off task and talking." (Yes, these are his words. Can you tell I groomed them well?) "Tomorrow we need to create peace by whispering and helping our partner who is beside us if they get stuck.

We don't want Ms. Askew to be all chaotic with her group in the back."

To say I was one proud teacher, would be a complete undercut to the growth my students had worked so hard to achieve that year. I was reminded at that moment, that I was truly fulfilling Kingdom work. In Matthew 5:9 Our Father says, "Blessed are the peacemakers, for they shall be called sons of God." I was developing a force of peacemakers that would one day go out and make a huge impression on the world! How simple, yet catalytic is that? Couldn't it be that simple? Could it really just take a few family meetings in one classroom to completely shift culture?

As you begin your day, think about what you feel brewing on the inside of you. Do you feel a sense of peace or chaos? Remember peace is your birthright, and thus you need to be intentional about protecting it and also recognizing when it is on the verge of being compromised.

Don't allow students, administration, test scores, meetings, or to do lists steal your peace. Quiet your mind and heart and focus on that which is within your locus of control. You can only do the best you know how with the resources you currently have. Take a deep breath and keep climbing. You are changing the world one class family meeting at a time.

Notes For the Day:

-Romans 4:19 So then we pursue the things which make for peace and the building up of one another.

-1 Peter 3:11 Turn away from evil and do good. Search for peace, and work to maintain it.

-Isaiah 55:12 You will go out in joy and be led forth in peace; the mountains and hills will burst into song before you, and all the trees of the field will clap their hands.

Homework:

Write down 3 ways you maintained your peace today.

_____

_____

_____

_____

_____

_____

_____

_____

_____

_____

_____

_____

_____

_____

_____

_____

_____

_____

_____

LESSON THIRTEEN

INTERVENTION

One school year I received a new student. Big deal you say? I received this student in April, only weeks before two state standardized tests. Not uncommon you say? Well, how about this student came from two doors down the hallway in another classroom? I know. Go ahead and gasp!

To make a long story short, this student was moved into my room because he displayed repetitive behavior issues that most times left him in the front office. I wasn't privy to this student, but apparently, all of the students, teachers, and administration were keenly aware of his behavior history.

I went to speak with the young man prior to him transitioning to our class family, just to let him know my expectations. Furthermore, I needed to wrap my mind around just what type of force was getting ready to enter my classroom. Who likes to be blindsided? Uhhh…not me! I'd worked incredibly hard to establish my current classroom culture. In contrast to all of the stories I'd heard about him, he appeared to be a well-behaved child. At least in those five minutes that I spoke with him.

The day came when I introduced him to our class family and made it clear my expectations for my students to help him incorporate peacefully. Of course, my students were eager to take on the task, but they knew Ricky's behavior streak from prior P.E., recess, and lunchtimes. I imagine they were wondering how many hours he would last in our classroom before I exposed the "mother" in me.

As time went on, I noticed that Ricky exemplified some of the best behavior in the classroom, and he even went out of his way to show a "caring heart," one of the hallmark behaviors of integrating into our class family well. Anytime I would frequent the front office, or even as I was meandering down the halls, without fail, someone would stop me to ask how Ricky was doing. My reply was always the same. "He's doing excellently!" They would look at me puzzled and walk off. Sheeeshh! What kind of history did this kid really have? Was I about to open Pandora's box?

During this time, I also noticed that Ricky didn't know how to read. Ok, hit the panic bottom! With only a few weeks left before our standardized tests, I wondered how this was even going to be possible for him. I also vacillated between the frustration and confusion of how he even made it to this grade and what was realistically expected of me at this point since he transitioned to my classroom that late in the year.

Most of all, I wondered how this student ever lived up to the talk that preceded him. He was such a sweet young man with me. Although he was incredibly low academically, he put forth so much effort to learn every day. He tracked me during all of the lessons, attempted to answer questions even when they were above his current capacity, loved on his class family, always tried to help other students resolve conflicts, and always made sure I understood he really appreciated me.

Ricky showed me what happens when "love" intervenes in our story. I don't know what happened when Ricky was in his other classroom. I can only speculate and contemplate the hearsay of others. What I do know is all I did was continue operating my class with structure, discipline, respect, joy, and love. I loved Ricky into his evolution, and he did just that. He evolved effortlessly. I didn't judge or scold him because he couldn't read. I didn't reprimand or embarrass him because he was still learning addition and subtraction, while the rest of the class was on division. All I did was meet him where he was, and I loved him into his development.

Love has a way of changing human beings effortlessly. In that short period of time, I was reminded of how Our Father comes into each of our lives, meets us exactly where we are, and loves us into our maturity. He doesn't condemn us for all of our sins and shortcomings. He doesn't point his finger at us because we are behind schedule in comparison to other human beings. He simply intervenes with love, calls us His own, and encourages us as we expand into the best version of ourselves. Don't you just love interventions?

Notes For the Day:

-*Ecclesiastes 9:11 Again I saw that under the sun the race is not to the swift, nor the battle to the strong, nor bread to the wise, nor riches to the intelligent, nor favor to those with knowledge, but time and chance happen to them all.*

-*Romans 5:8 But God shows his love for us in that while we were still sinners, Christ died for us.*

-John 8:7 So when they continued asking Him, He lifted Himself up and said unto them, "He that is without sin among you, let him first cast a stone at her."

Homework:

Stage a compassion intervention for one of your students. Who is the student? How are you going to meet them where they are and support them on their progress trail?

_____

_____

_____

_____

_____

_____

_____

_____

_____

_____

_____

_____

_____

_____

_____

_____

LESSON FOURTEEN

GUIDANCE

Do you realize that you've been called to guide the next generation in a way that prepares them to be impactful, influential, & purposefully positive as they mature into adults? I thought I'd just drop that bomb on you and get it over with for now. Ha! Truly, that is the essence of what you are called to do as a teacher. You are charged daily with the responsibility of guiding undeveloped minds to a specific level of refinement with the help of the Holy Spirit.

At the start of each school year, I've always found myself creating vision and goals for my kids to attain. One consistent goal I've perpetually had is for the classroom to be student-led. This basically means that my students are able to function and operate in the classroom as a micro society with me only stepping in to facilitate the "hard spots." No this hasn't been an attempt for me to have the luxury of sitting behind my desk as my students "do school." In fact, I can count on one hand the number of times I've sat behind my desk in a classroom filled with kids.

Instead, this has been my goal because I know it is necessary that my students are able to operate on the level of their micro society- their little realm of the world, effectively and at their highest capability with minimal input from me, in order to progress into adults who lead with integrity. Let me lend you an example.

Conflict resolution is something that I place great emphasis on in my classrooms. One day, my students came back from recess and apparently there were several small conflicts that transpired that were not resolved by a witnessing adult. I could tell something strange had ensued when I saw the hands shoot up in the air like rockets upon entering the building. With a quick gesture, I signaled to my students to put their hands down and wait until we were back in the classroom so we could discuss it.

Let's be honest, who wants a stampede of children thronging you right after you've just scarfed down your food in the allotted 30 minutes (or less) prescribed for lunch? Can I try to digest my food first and then put my teacher hat back on? Oh the joys of teaching.

A bathroom break later, we entered the room and I rolled my chair to the middle of the classroom and sat down. You could hear an ant's tears falling in that place! I directed two students who were involved in the incidents to begin speaking one at a time. The only time I involved myself in the conversation was to pause a child if they happened to speak at the same time another child was talking. I wanted them to understand the importance of the power in their words as well as the intentionality of honoring their classmates' words.

I continued to sit and listen as my students poured their hearts out to one another. Frustrations flew, pain could be felt, embarrassment evolved, and disappointment darted to and fro. In the next few moments, I did something no teacher in her sane mind would have done. I stepped away and just observed like a mama giraffe watching her calves attempting to walk after the tenth failed attempt.

What happened in the next ten minutes melted my heart like chocolatey smores resting on teddy bear colored graham crackers at a fireside camp. I observed as all of my training I'd poured into my students was activated without me. Let it be known that the Word doesn't lie when it says in Proverbs 22:6, "Train up a child in the way he should go: and when he is old, he will not depart from it."

Right before my eyes, my students began to break out of their molds and showcase the leadership and conflict resolution skills that'd been stewing behind the masks of their little kid bodies. I was elated! I didn't step in once to help them. I watched as they corralled in the back of the classroom using their words, waiting respectfully for others to finish speaking, offering solutions sets, persevering through the agitation, only to arrive at an amicable solution that everyone agreed upon. I watched them exchange apologizes, hugs, and handshakes to indicate forgiveness and restoration. My heart smiled.

It's in those times when we are ready to call it quits because we assume everything we say to our students flies right over their heads, that they show up to prove us wrong. Your guidance matters. Whether your students appear to be listening or not, trust that your words, teaching methods, modeling, and facilitation are sticking to their core like gum in a toddler's hair. When you place them in situations where they are forced to be activated, they will rise to the occasion. Guide them well teacher. Shepherd them well because soon you will be tasked to let them go. You'll have to trust that what you've sown so diligently in them will break through the epidermal layer of society dictating that they remain kids until they are "old enough" for their voices to be heard. Lead them well teacher and scaffold that release of control. They will rise every time!

Notes For the Day:

-John 14:26 But the Advocate, the Holy Spirit, whom the Father will send in my name, will teach you all things and will remind you of everything I have said to you.

-John 3:30 He must become greater; I must become less.

-1 Timothy 4:12 Don't let anyone look down on you because you are young, but set an example for the believers in speech, in conduct, in love, in faith and in purity.

Homework:

Look for an opportunity today to release control over your students so they can navigate the area where you have previously provided guidance. How did it turn out?

_____

_____

_____

_____

_____

_____

_____

_____

_____

_____

_____

_____

LESSON FIFTEEN

VULNERABILITY

Yayyyyyy!!! It was the end of the school year! We made it! Well…almost. It was field trip day, so I'd say that's close enough. Surprisingly, field trip day was one of my favorite days of the entire school year. No, not because I need to keep a magnifying glass on each child's behavior or make sure that a child doesn't get lost, sick, or kidnapped in the process. Ha! It was actually my favorite day because I felt this was the day I could let my hair down, somewhat slide to the left of my teacher hat, and just have fun with my kids. After all, we'd worked our bottoms off! I'd pretty much tapped out at this point in the year. K-O!

This particular field trip was like none of the others I'd taken during my teaching pilgrimage. Shall I set the scene yet again? I had this one specific student, who from the onset of the year, vied to make me lose my passion, love, and care to see her excel. The year prior, had been dubbed her worst school year yet! She'd lost her mother tragically and began to express herself in violence, self-defense, and constant rebellion towards any authority figure. That was until she met her match.....me.

From the day I met Sierra, I knew she was going to be one I'd take under my wing. She needed tough love and a whole lot of it. Tough because that was her disposition and love because at her core she was screaming for someone or something to heal the wounds within her. Needless to say, I was told not a single day went by without her being in the principal's office the previous year.

Somewhere within the first five conversations I ever had with Sierra, I told her she would never go the principal's office on my watch. EVER! We would settle every issue in the classroom as a family should. Side note: at the beginning of each year, I established the understanding that my students were not just students attending school, but we were all now a member of a class family.

Throughout the year, Sierra had her moments. My goodness did she have myriad of them! However, that didn't stop me from keeping my word. She was going to have to override my feistiness and zeal for educating kids if she was going to win this battle. Trust me, I wasn't going to let that happen. Can you tell I'm a spunky teacher?

Field trip day arrived. It was a hard-pressed situation even supporting this young lady to the finish line of being permitted to attend. Let's just say, she really had to earn this trip! We were walking around the mini theme park headed to the race cars and all of a sudden I felt someone grab my hand. Mind you, my students were way past the age of wanting to hold an adult's hand, so I was a little shocked. To my surprise when I glimpsed down, Sierra was holding my hand and saying, "Come on Ms. Askew, can you ride the race cars with me?"

Ouuuuweeeeee!! You could only imagine the facial expression that I suppressed. Could this truly be the young lady, who constantly wanted to fight other students, challenge every adult authority, and gain the badge for being "The Most Troubled Student in the School?" No way! Oddly enough, there she was showing up so innocent and so vulnerable. My heart melted like butter in a cast iron skillet.

That day, I had two choices. I could have ignored Sierra and recounted the number of times she made me work for my paycheck, or I could let down my guard, welcome vulnerability, and meet her in a moment that she'd yearned on having her entire life. I chose the latter. Sierra gave me an opportunity to see myself through Our Heavenly Father's eyes. How many times have you and I messed up? How many times have we been disobedient to what Our Father tells us to do and instead we commence to doing life our way?

Despite our shortcomings, how many times does Our Father forgive us and welcome us into a space to be intimate with Him in the name of vulnerability? Too many to even cite. He allows us to let our guards down and showcase our real hearts with Him, even though He knows us anyway. Allowing "us" to lead our vulnerability is powerful! There isn't a moment where He judges, condemns, or reminds us of all we've down wrong. He simply accepts and loves us. He meets us where we are emotionally and mentally, and proceeds to restore us back to our true identity: children of the Most High God.

Today take time to notice when your students are extending the invitation for you to be vulnerable with them. Sometimes it's necessary to take off the teacher hat and simply meet them as a human being of wisdom in a place where they can be unashamed and repentant through their actions more so than their words.

Notes For the Day:

-1 Corinthians 2:3-4 I came to you in weakness and fear, and with much trembling and my speech and my message were not in plausible words of wisdom, but in demonstration of the Spirit and of power.

-Colossians 1:22 Yet now he has reconciled you to himself through the death of Christ in his physical body. As a result, he has brought you into his own presence, and you are holy and blameless as you stand before him without a single fault.

-John 8:7 And as they continued to ask him, he stood up and said to them, "Let him who is without sin among you be the first to throw a stone at her."

Homework:

As a teacher, what does vulnerability look like in your classroom?

_____

_____

_____

_____

_____

_____

_____

_____

_____

_____

_____

_____

Week 4

LESSON SIXTEEN

COMPASSION

I never quite understood compassion until I worked in departmentalized settings. This particular year, I was teaching my homeroom kids all subjects expect math, and I was teaching two classes of reading to fulfill my work schedule. Of course this was also a year where my students had to take three state standardized tests! You're not surprised right?

As the year kicked off, I was filled with an enthusiasm to tackle the world! My brain was bulging with ideas to bring joy in the classroom, make the journey to the exams a seamless one, and on top of that I had all of these really innovative ideas I wanted to try out on my students for reading lessons.

As the year progressed, the complexities of school started to weigh on me. You know what I'm talking about. Student behavior that makes you want to pluck your eyelashes out, test scores fluctuating to the geographic epicenters, and administrative pressures of adding several cherries on the top of your already toppling ice cream cone of things to do!

I tried to remain as optimistic as possible because hope is the base of my personality. I cling on to hope like a pit bull with lockjaw! Day by day, I found myself having to pause at my desk and feed myself the scriptures I'd hung behind me to remind me of why I was in that classroom, what my assignment was, and how My Creator is with me every single step of the way.

On one such day, I had a conversation. Let's be honest. It was more like a vent session, with one of my team teachers. After I'd word vomited on him my disappointments and frustrations and connected all of that to what Our Heavenly Father had been telling me, I supposed if nothing else, I got it all off my chest.

The next morning I walked into class about 30 minutes earlier just to get my bearings together and prepare for the day. To my surprise, my co-worker was walking in to hand me an envelope. I didn't think too much of it until I saw my name on it. I looked up quite puzzled because after all it wasn't my birthday.

I proceeded to open the envelope which exposed a humorous card along with scripture written on the inside of it. The card spoke to my frustration I unleashed the previous day and it reminded me of who I was as a child of God. It was full of encouraging scriptures that proclaimed my strength and my identity as an overcomer.

As the school year continued to unfold, every now and then, I retrieved that card which was proof that Our Father hears our cries and sees when things get tough in our lives. He dispatches His angels in an effort to sustain us. Oh, what compassion He bestows upon us!

Today may have started off rough for you. I encourage you to lift your head and be in expectation of Our Father's compassion towards you through a human being. Perhaps it'll come from a lunch monitor, an appreciation text via a parent, through a custodian, or simply through one of your student's big bear hugs. Trust me. He sees when your heart is sad, and He always does something about it. The compassion of the Christ.

Notes For Day:

-Matthew 4:11 Then the devil left him, and angels came and attended him.

-Isaiah 30:18 Yet the LORD longs to be gracious to you; therefore he will rise up to show you compassion. For the LORD is a God of justice. Blessed are all who wait for him!

-Isaiah 54:10 Though the mountains be shaken and the hills be removed, yet my unfailing love for you will not be shaken nor my covenant of peace be removed," says the LORD, who has compassion on you.

Homework:

Commit to one act of showing compassion to one coworker you see who is struggling. Write down the coworkers name and plan a simple act of compassion.

_____

_____

_____

_____

_____

_____

LESSON SEVENTEEN

HUMILITY

The classroom is arguably one of the best places to practice humility. In a school, isn't everyone supposed to be a student? A school is an institution founded on information acquisition. In other words, everyone in the building should be positioned as a "learner" whether you are a child or an adult.

In my attempt to develop my students into fearless little people who delight in making mistakes in order to truly find their sweet spot of what sets their little hearts ablaze, I found myself consistently eating the largest slices of humble pie. I must say, there is such freedom in making mistakes and being ok with outcomes not producing as you predicted.

I had one such child who couldn't stand being wrong. Anytime Steven would miss a question or fail to use the correct punctuation, it would spill out of him in the form of frustration and self-condemnation. As I observed his behavior patterns, I couldn't help but wonder what made him feel like he had to be perfect? In those moments, I saw myself in Steven. I saw the many times I refrained from doing something new only because I hadn't studied it and showed myself to have expertise in that specific area.

Wow! How many opportunities have we missed to discover our strengths and weaknesses because we shield ourselves under the guise of perfection? Everyone knows that there is no perfect person in and of themselves on this planet. That is, unless you are a robot or alien. Or you just happen to be King Jesus himself. I figured no hands would go up on that one.

That's the narrative I began to tell my students to support them in loosening their grip on this unhealthy need and desire to always be correct. During lessons, I would find ways to purposely make mistakes, just so I could model to my students how to walk through them and still come out on the other side victorious and wise because they learned what did and did not work.

For some reason, I began to enjoy those parts of my lesson way too much. I would make mistakes writing on the board, errors in answering math questions, and even blunders in simply being an adult. I wanted to ingrain in their hearts the fact that being humble and positioning your heart to learn, is one of the most powerful stances they'll ever have access to in their lives. When you are able to admit you are wrong, acknowledge you don't have it all figured out, apologize to others, and be teachable, that is when you are harnessing your power at its zenith.

It's no wonder I had so much fun being vulnerable in front of my students. We live in a world where as you mature into an adult, it's no longer acceptable for you to show your humanity i.e. your ineptness. Yet in the Kingdom of God isn't that precisely what He tells us to do? Proverbs 1:7 tells us, "The fear of the Lord is the beginning of knowledge; fools despise wisdom and instruction." We should all start taking our slice of humble pie. Physical growth is inevitable, but in order to grow intrinsically, we need to tap into Our Father's knowledge.

Go out into the world today and admit you don't know all the answers, but you'll be resourceful and try to find out. Confess that you don't have your entire life figured out, but you know The One who does. Affirm that you make mistakes and apologize when it affects someone. Take risks when it's not guaranteed that you'll excel. Trust that you serve a God who promises to never leave you nor forsake you, has already forgiven you, and will be there to pick you up when you miss the mark. He will always correct you in love. Go for it! Take heart! Be humble! You'll be surprised at the outcome.

Notes For the Day:

-James 4:6 But he gives us more grace. That is why Scripture says: "God opposes the proud but shows favor to the humble.

-Luke 14:11 For all those who exalt themselves will be humbled, and those who humble themselves will be exalted."

-2 Corinthians 12:9-10 But he said to me, "My grace is sufficient for you, for my power is made perfect in weakness." Therefore I will boast all the more gladly about my weaknesses, so that Christ's power may rest on me. That is why, for Christ's sake, I delight in weaknesses, in insults, in hardships, in persecutions, in difficulties. For when I am weak, then I am strong.

Homework:

Find one opportunity to humble yourself in a faculty or PLC meeting this week. Write about how it turned out.

_____

_____

_____

_____

_____

_____

_____

_____

_____

_____

_____

_____

_____

_____

_____

_____

_____

_____

LESSON EIGHTEEN

BATTLES

My first year of teaching was horrible! At least that's how I felt. I cried more days than I could count and quite frankly I contemplated packing my bags for good during dismissal each day. Put one hand up if your first year of teaching was amazing. I salute you! Truly you are the REAL MVP!

My introduction into the world of teaching was met with children who were three grades below their expected academic level, non-compliant students, unorganized lesson plans, a lack of administrative and parental support, and an uneasiness surrounding how to navigate this new realm. Teaching wasn't my first career. It was actually my third, and it packed its own round of punches that didn't even exist in my other professions.

I would describe my first year of teaching as "battle tested." It almost seems like the world of education throws every weapon imaginable at you in order to see how well you can dodge and handle the intensities of the profession. My question was always: Where was the warm-up round??

I learned one major lesson that year. In addition to discovering that staying at work until 7 pm every night isn't going to help you, I learned that some seasons are lined with battles. Battles that will attempt to wreck your spirit and literally take you out of the game.

Yes, children will misbehave, deadlines will pile on top of you like stacks of dirty laundry, administration will always be in your midst with a magnifying glass, parents will sometimes believe you are the root cause of the problem, children just will not understand some lessons, and you will have to repeat yourself a billion times before actual learning begins to occur. However, one thing will always remain true. When you fight all of your battles on your knees in prayer, you will win EVERYTIME!

Prayer fortifies us to accomplish what we could never accomplish on our own. When we surrender to our methods of fighting battles, and we simply pray and then put one foot in front of the other to collaborate with Our Father, miracles happen.

As you are preparing to open your classroom door and greet your students, take a few minutes and ask Our Father to strengthen you for the battle that lays ahead. Thank Him in advance for your victory. Now open that door with your battle gear on, love on your kids, and teach your heart out! This victory is certain and this battle is the Lord's.

Notes For the Day:

-2 Chronicles 20:15 He said: "Listen, King Jehoshaphat and all who live in Judah and Jerusalem! This is what the LORD says to you: 'Do not be afraid or discouraged because of this vast army. For the battle is not yours, but God's.'

-2 Corinthians 10: 3-5 For though we live in the world, we do not wage war as the world does. The weapons we fight with are not the weapons of the world. On the contrary, they have divine power to demolish strongholds. We demolish arguments and every pretension that sets itself up against the knowledge of God, and we take captive every thought to make it obedient to Christ.

-Ephesians 6: 11-17 Put on the full armor of God, so that you can take your stand against the devil's schemes. For our struggle is not against flesh and blood, but against the rulers, against the authorities, against the powers of this dark world and against the spiritual forces of evil in the heavenly realms. Therefore put on the full armor of God, so that when the day of evil comes, you may be able to stand your ground, and after you have done everything, to stand. Stand firm then, with the belt of truth buckled around your waist, with the breastplate of righteousness in place, and with your feet fitted with the readiness that comes from the gospel of peace. In addition to all this, take up the shield of faith, with which you can extinguish all the flaming arrows of the evil one. Take the helmet of salvation and the sword of the Spirit, which is the word of God.

Homework:

Write out those things that you see as battles in your life today. Now give them to Our Heavenly Father. Let them go. Let Him announce your victory.

_____

_____

_____

_____

_____

_____

_____

_____

_____

_____

_____

_____

_____

_____

_____

_____

_____

LESSON NINETEEN

STRENGTH

It was my second year in the teaching profession and somehow I'd decided that me taking the leap to join an expedited Master in Education program was the best thing for me to do. Do you recall me telling you that I cried almost every day during my first year of teaching? Yea, so it only makes sense that I'd want to overload my plate my second year of teaching right? Oh me. My discernment and my common sense decided to partner up and vacate the premises at the same time. Or did they?

Til this day, I don't know what brought me to the conclusion that I should tackle an advanced degree while being a full-time teacher, especially after seeing how my first year of teaching went. Oh, and did I mention I was surplussed at the beginning of this particular year? More specifically, I was moved to a brand-new school after teaching one month of kindergarten. I was reassigned as a 5th-grade teacher. You got it! Another testing year. Is it me or do I see a pattern?

Nonetheless, let the full-time expedited graduate student and full time teacher life begin! Ha! Oddly enough, that memorable school year, I found an amazing groove. I'd begun planning my lessons out 3 weeks in advance and even had a grip on the task I loathe the most which is... grading papers! I was leaving work no more than 30 minutes after dismissal, and I was doing all of that while going to school at night in classes that didn't end until 10 pm! Did I mention my bedtime was 10 pm? You might as well call me Cinderella because when the clock strikes 10, I'm in the land of zzzzzzzzs. I'm gone to visit the field of my dreams cuddled up in my best sleep. In addition to that, my workout regimen was the best it'd been in years! My first year of teaching I gained 12 pounds! My second year I'd lost more than 12 pounds the healthy way. You go girl!

As it approached graduation day, all I could do was look back on what had to have been my Heavenly Father's strength waxing strong in me. No one came and took away the problems that the education system presented. It was all still there. The students, the parents, the standardized tests, the to-do lists, the afterschool tutoring, and this expedited graduate program to top it all off. I was writing papers, presenting my thesis, you know...all the work that comes with a graduate program.

Yet, by His grace and nothing else, He made all of it seem "just breezy." I was astonished and full of thanksgiving. What is that thing that is on your heart that you want to do, but have no clue how you're going to do it? Pray about it, and if He tells you to go for it, then do it! Don't talk yourself out of it because it sounds absurd or irrational. Most of what Our Father tells us to do doesn't make sense to us anyway. Interestingly enough, He always has a way of working things out beautifully.

Be encouraged! He is not looking for your strength. He will be the strength on the inside of you. Walk boldly and let Him take the reins. Taste and see that He is so good!

Notes For the Day:

-Psalm 34:8 *Taste and see that the Lord is good; blessed is the one who takes refuge in him.*

-2 Corinthians 12: 9-11 *But he said to me, "My grace is sufficient for you, for my power is made perfect in weakness." Therefore I will boast all the more gladly about my weaknesses, so that Christ's power may rest on me. That is why, for Christ's sake, I delight in weaknesses, in insults, in hardships, in persecutions, in difficulties. For when I am weak, then I am strong.*

-Isaiah 40:31 *but those who hope in the LORD will renew their strength. They will soar on wings like eagles; they will run and not grow weary, they will walk and not be faint.*

Homework:

What area of work do you need to release to Him today so He can be strong in you?

_____

_____

_____

_____

_____

_____

_____

_____

LESSON TWENTY

JOY

Some of the greatest moments you'll ever experience this school year are when you lean into the "joy" your students create. Society tells us that once we are adults, all the silliness needs to go out the window and seriousness needs to become our disposition. Yet didn't Our Father say in Matthew 18:3, "Truly I tell you, unless you change and become like little children, you will never enter the kingdom of heaven?

Now I'm not advocating for adults to become "childish," rather I'm reminding you of the attitude of faith that Our Father directed us to have. Have you ever noticed that children find joy in the most random places? It's their nature. They view the world a lot more simply than us adults do.

There were so many times in class when my students burst out laughing at a line in the chapter book we were reading or collectively cackled when one of the students laughed at themselves while mispronouncing a word. It was almost as though the hysterical laughter was contagious. It would start with one student trying to hold their breath, and it would soon domino and ricochet around the classroom without fail.

I found myself during these times, not scolding my students for being off task, but just being present and observing them in the moment. My heartstrings were so familiar with the freedom of laughing and enjoying the moment in wonderous giggles. These nostalgic moments crept up on me in ways I couldn't even anticipate in the classroom. These junctures brought me back to my humanity and out of the "teacher trap" of performance.

There's something about hearing children laugh that makes a breach in a lesson so necessary. It's even better when you let go to join in. Give it a try. The next time you catch your students getting ready to swallow the biggest belly roar of a laugh, crack a smile to let them know it's ok. Then chime in with them. Watch their faces light up when they realize that you too are still a human being who finds humor in the silly moments.

Sometimes we just need to stop taking ourselves and life so seriously and reap the strength that comes from being joyful. Being too rigid will hinder you from the renewal that one receives from joy. With that being said, laugh to your heart's content and do it with your students because it will make it that much more special.

Notes For the Day:

-*Nehemiah 8:10 10 Nehemiah said, "Go and enjoy choice food and sweet drinks, and send some to those who have nothing prepared. This day is holy to our Lord. Do not grieve, for the joy of the LORD is your strength."*

-Philippians 4:4 Rejoice in the Lord always. I will say it again: Rejoice!

-1 Thessalonians 5:16-18 Rejoice always, pray continually, give thanks in all circumstances; for this is God's will for you in Christ Jesus.

Homework:

Choose joy today! What is something that makes you smile from the inside out? Do that thing and enjoy yourself! You deserve it!

_____

_____

_____

_____

_____

_____

_____

_____

_____

_____

_____

_____

_____

_____

_____

Week 5

LESSON TWENTY-ONE

MIGHT

Make no mistake about it. Teaching is a strenuous job. Although it doesn't appear to be physically demanding, it is spiritually, emotionally, and relationally taxing. It demands from you qualities you are forced to unearth that you never even realized lay dormant beneath the surface of your personality.

There are days when I would go to work and I knew simply being present was the greatest service I could give that day. I had no fight left in me, but I honored my portion enough to say, "I'm going to show up." Some would question why you should even show up if you're maxed out. I agree with that to the extent that you are not claiming to be maxed out the majority of the school year. By all means, take care of yourself, implement healthy boundaries, and call in a substitute when you need to do so.

On the contrary, I'm speaking about those days when you simply don't feel like mustering up the courage to execute any lesson plans. Recall with me if you will what Our Father said in Zechariah 4:6, "So he said to me, "This is the word of the LORD to Zerubbabel: 'Not by might nor by power, but by my Spirit,' says the LORD Almighty." Your ability and effectiveness is not what landed you on Planet Education. Our Father did. Neither will your strength equip you to accomplish all He's called you to do and be as a teacher.

Arrive at school a tad bit earlier than you normally do. Go through the motions if you must to get into the building, but when you get in your classroom, pause for a moment. Tell Your Father who yearns to hear from you, just how exhausted you are. Tell Him how you'd like nothing better than to be pulling the blankets up around your neck right now. Tell Him how you are empty and don't even have a smile to pay your students. Then quiet your soul and allow Him to send His angels to minister to your spirit just like they ministered to Jesus after He was tempted for 40 days and 40 nights in Matthew 4:11.

Allow His words to quiet you. Confess the scriptures below aloud.

Notes For the Day:

> - *Zephaniah 3:17 The LORD your God is in your midst, a mighty one who will save; he will rejoice over you with gladness; he will quiet you by his love; he will exult over you with loud singing.*

> -*1 Peter 5:10 In His kindness God called me to share in His eternal glory by means of Christ Jesus. So after I have suffered a little while, He will restore, support, and strengthen me, and He will place me on a firm foundation.*

> -*Ephesians 3:20 Now all glory to God, who is able, through his mighty power at work within me, to accomplish infinitely more than I might ask or think.*

Homework:

Search out two more scriptures that testify to God's strength coming alive in you to do what you cannot do. Use these for your confessions tomorrow.

_____

_____

_____

_____

_____

_____

_____

_____

_____

_____

_____

_____

_____

_____

_____

_____

_____

_____

_____

LESSON TWENTY-TWO

ENDURANCE

To say that teaching is a profession that attempts to deplete you like a teenager drains the battery on a cell phone is an understatement! The number of hats that a teacher must wear is unprecedented! You need to manage the lives of upwards of 25 students. Oh and let's not forget that includes intervening to help them navigate home life, their educational attainment, as well as the joys and complexities of what it means to be a human being simply living life. You need to take attendance, differentiate your lessons to accommodate the needs of all children, attend RTI, ARD, PLC, and SPED meetings, let alone keep up with the mile high list of acronyms that correspond to the field. You must attend faculty meetings, participate in before and after school duty, grade papers, scarf down your food in less than 30 minutes, put a complete halt on your body's bowel movement system, and prepare report cards and progress/interim reports!

In addition, you need to chaperone school dances, complete cum files, decorate your classroom, analyze data, tutor your students, attend literacy, math, and science nights, prepare awards for ceremonies, oh and I forgot the most important task of them all......you actually need to teach your kids! After all, that is why you applied to be a teacher right? Trust me. I know exactly how teacher life is set up.

If you aren't careful and deliberate, you'll easily burn out of this profession in a matter of days. Let's not forget, some teachers actually have a personal life including family and friends outside the classroom. So how does one maintain in this profession? Do you just quit at the 199th tattle tale from your student? Do you throw in the towel after you've tutored the same child for six months but have yet to see their test score climb above the 60% mark? Do you faint when your administration adds another "action item" to your already explosive to-do list? I'm glad you inquired.

My answer: not at all. I remember the day I was so exhausted at work, I could fall asleep standing up. My battery was on empty. I stood behind my classroom door as the morning bell rang to indicate the start of the school day. How in the world was I going to pull this one off? My feet were planted on the geometric tile on my classroom floor in the dark (because we teachers keep the lights off in the morning to prepare the atmosphere for a calm day), with my arm extended towards the doorknob. I thought to myself, "There is no way, I am going to be able to perform today."

Let's be honest. Teaching is a full-scale production! From the moment the morning bell blares signaling the production is beginning, your job is to perform in such a way that ALL, and I mean ALL of your students are engaged and interacting with what you are serving the audience that day. You could be teaching them the life cycle for all anyone cares, but I bet by the end of the lesson, those animals will have somehow appeared in your classroom and given an entirely new meaning to the movie, "The Lion King." That's what passionate teachers do! We don't know anything else.

Back to my epic moment of standing at the door reaching for the handle. Can you imagine the camera crew panning in on the sound of my heartbeat, my smothered breathing rhythm, and tears that somehow remain caged in my body? Did I intrigue you with my drama yet? Ha!

At that moment, I heard Our Heavenly Father whisper to me to pray. "Talk to me daughter. Give me your cares. I called you to this profession for such a time as this, and I will see to it that you excel." I surrendered immediately. I let everything that was weighing me down flow from my mind, heart, and mouth. I relinquished it all to Him. I asked Him to help me with every detail of my work day. I appealed to Him for a strategy to speak to my students during the lessons. I even prayed over their minds and hearts to receive the atmosphere I'd set during my time of prayer. I confessed His strength over me as He fed me my true identity. In a matter of minutes, I was striding over to the door to open it with a vivacious smile on my face!

Prayer does change things. If you are hard pressed right now, take a moment to connect with Our Heavenly Father. Carve out the time to do it. It's imperative. A few minutes is all you need before the kids enter the class in the morning. Or, if that isn't a good time try using the time the kids are at P.E. or during lunch. You also can take 3 minutes from your planning period or you can even step in the doorway while your students are completing independent work to mutter a scripture to yourself that reminds you....you got this! You are not in that classroom by accident! You are graced to connect with these kids! Keep pressing!

Notes For the Day:

-Romans 12:12 Rejoice in hope, be patient in tribulation, be constant in prayer.

-Hebrews 10:36 You need to persevere so that when you have done the will of God, you will receive what he has promised.

-2 Corinthians 12:9-10 But he said to me, "My grace is sufficient for you, for my power is made perfect in weakness." Therefore I will boast all the more gladly of my weaknesses, so that the power of Christ may rest upon me. For the sake of Christ, then, I am content with weaknesses, insults, hardships, persecutions, and calamities. For when I am weak, then I am strong.

Homework:

Write out a prayer that you can confess when you feel like throwing in the teacher bag and leaving the classroom.

_____

_____

_____

_____

_____

_____

_____

_____

_____

_____

_____

LESSON TWENTY-THREE

FAITH

Let's have a moment of truth. After your first two weeks of teaching did you feel super qualified to attack the mission that was set ahead of you, or did you wonder who in the world thought it was a good idea to hire you for this position without adequate training? I shot my hand up at the latter! Let's face the facts. Your first couple of weeks and months in the classroom is simply survival mode. Although you prepared your lesson plans, a few teachers passed down some of their class library books, you have cute little labels posted strategically in the classroom, you have your daily agenda posted, you are wearing your fashionable teacher attire, you've sharpened a special pencil for each child, and your room color coordinates with your theme, you truly have no idea what is getting ready to unfold in the ensuing 10 months!

My advice is that you become fairly comfortable with the fact that you are dealing with small humans with fragile minds who have yet to meet the maturity level that society glorifies as year eighteen. The year they become full-fledged adults, full of wisdom, making every decision a wise one. Riiiggght, because we all know that when we become adults we've reached the zenith of human perfection? Ha! Hardly! If that was the case, even teachers would have answered the opening question to this chapter with the former response.

Don't beat yourself up. Understand that you've accepted the challenge better known as a "faith walk." Even Jesus, who was also a teacher, taught without the guarantee that His students, His disciples would embrace and retain all He was teaching them. He envisioned His disciples receiving His instruction, digesting it, applying it daily, and teaching it to others. I believe that was his prayer and hope. Yet, because He was also dealing with human beings who have free will, a hope and prayer are all it could be at best. To think that was Jesus' desire, and He was dealing with adults and not even children. I'd say you're in good company!

As you amble through the semesters, be conscious of this "faith walk." No, you are not going to be given the blueprint and script of what this entire year will entail, nor will you be able to foresee the complexities of your students' behaviors. However, you will be expected to continue to put one foot in front of the other. You must trust and believe that your teaching is sticking with your students, that they will apply it daily as you add more skills to their memory set, and that they will teach their peers.

None of that is guaranteed. Your students may choose to be off task for 3 months of the school year. They may choose to only apply a portion of what you've taught. They may unfortunately, lack the foundation for you to build on at all.

Having an understanding of all of these scenarios, you are still tasked to prepare in the best way you know how for your students. Commit to greeting them joyfully at the start of each school day, loving and supporting them in their development, and having faith that the results will yield a measure of success for each child. I'd be lying if I said the road was easy, but when is achieving something valuable ever easy?

When Jesus was preparing to meet death in Matthew 26:41 the Word says, "Then he returned to his disciples and found them sleeping. "Couldn't you men keep watch with me for one hour?" he asked Peter. "Watch and pray so that you will not fall into temptation. The spirit is willing, but the flesh is weak." Jesus instructed them to stay awake, trusting that'd they'd apply what He told them. Yet, His disciples fell asleep three times! Wow! Talk about not following directions!

What I am saying is, be gentle with yourself. Even Jesus' students had trouble applying what He was teaching. Don't you remember Matthew 24:29 when Jesus says, "Come. Then Peter got down out of the boat, walked on the water and came toward Jesus." Don't forget about the part when Peter took his eyes off Jesus and became afraid. Your students will not get it right every time. They just won't, and that ok because neither will you. Do your best to prepare for them, and then put one foot in front of the other, "faith walking" your way through the school year. I promise as you are walking, you'll start to see manifestations of some of the things you prayed about before you ever took your first step. Walk it out!

Notes For the Day:

-2 Corinthians 5:7 For we live by faith, not by sight.

-James 2:26 For as the body apart from the spirit is dead, so also faith apart from works is dead.

-Hebrews 11:6 And without faith it is impossible to please him, for whoever would draw near to God must believe that he exists and that he rewards those who seek him.

Homework:

Set your timer and prepare for the lessons you will teach tomorrow. Once your timer blares, thank your Father for helping you curate a tailored lesson plan. Give Him the remainder of your cares. Write your cares down here, let them go, and in the morning begin your daily "faith walk." I believe in you!

_____

_____

_____

_____

_____

_____

_____

_____

_____

_____

_____

_____

_____

_____

_____

_____

LESSON TWENTY-FOUR

DISCERNMENT

If you haven't experienced it yet, you'll soon learn that your discernment will take you a long way as an educator. When you are responsible for upwards of 28 students a day, you must have access to some type of supernatural ability that will allow you to serve efficiently and effectively. Without it… I cringe, and say, good luck!

When you employ Biblical discernment, you allow the Holy Spirit to lead and give you direction on a matter. Otherwise, you're operating in your limited knowledge and rationale. Discernment can help you gauge when a student is listening to you, but not hearing you. It helps you to take deeper steps to understand if your student is being abused at home. It aids you in determining the direct spot you should pick up in a lesson that you didn't finish teaching the previous day. It assists you in asking your student questions that may lead to the knowledge that he/she is being bullied. I even use it to identify students who are tempted to cheat during assessments.

Discernment plays a great role in helping you navigate as a teacher. Imagine being on a field trip and not having the discernment to tell you that one of your students needs to slow down their breathing because they are on the verge of an asthma attack! Once you get a hold of your ability to discern, your life will forever be changed!

I recall a time when I had a student who had a tendency towards emotional breakdowns, threatening of suicide, and unyielded anger in any given moment. He was also diagnosed with several mental illnesses. At the parent's request, this child was placed on medication. Still, my responsibility was to love this child into his maturity and help him navigate his personality at his current age, with or without medicine.

Thankfully my ability to discern was heightened one particular day that school year. That morning, my student entered the classroom a little differently. To the untrained eye, you probably would have thought he was just being his normal self. I knew better. There was something very different about his presence even though he hadn't said or done anything unusual.

As the day progressed, I knew it was necessary to keep an eye on Him. The still small voice of Our Father on the inside of me told me so. As I continued to teach the lesson, I noticed he somewhat blanked out. It was almost like he mentally left the classroom. I continued to teach the lesson as normal and signaled to one of my students to go next door and ask the teacher to step into the hallway for a moment. Mind you, all of my students were still behaving normally at this point. However, I was setting up a protection system for my kids in the event, the next few minutes went downhill as I was sensing it would.

By the time my student returned from the hallway, Craig had stood up and was headed towards the door. I quickly redirected him calmly, so as to not make a scene. This wasn't a moment for your normal redirection or reminder of who the authority was in the room. This was something that could prove to be dangerous! Thankfully I knew that, and I also knew how to handle what was about to happen.

I'd already trained my students pretty well on what to do, should something like this ever occur. (The culture that I'd established in my classroom was one in which we all had an understanding of nuances, tendencies, patterns, and fluctuations of each child. We were a classroom family, and so we learned each other very well. We also learned how to respect the differences of each child and how to honor the current development level of each child. I promise it's not as hard to teach it to your kids as it sounds. Ha!)

I'll fast forward the story a bit. At this point, my students were all being taken care of by another adult. I was in the stairwell with Craig who was holding on to a balcony threatening to end his life! How could a child have mentally gathered this plan? Your guess is as good as mine. Let's just say I'm so thankful for the Holy Spirit who led me in a way that was able to keep my entire class safe from harm and exposure to such behavior. Also, thanks to the Holy Spirit, I was able to talk Craig out of his intentions in the presence of his mother. That is, after we chased him down the street! Yes, a chase! I didn't know when I signed up to be a classroom teacher, I'd also need to be able to prove my physical stamina against a child who could clearly outrun me in a relay race any day. Ha!

I digress. That day, I received an endowment of supernatural power, and let's not forget the help of a co-worker's vehicle. My goodness did I work for my paycheck that day! I mention all of this not to create a humorous or tragic picture, but rather to showcase the power of the Holy Spirit filling you with discernment to show up as the best educator that you possibly can. I thank Our Father so much for the sparing of this child's life and for giving me the ability to surrender to the Holy Spirit that day. Without it, Craig's story could have ended very differently.

Take a moment today to tap into what Our Father may be showing you. Then be bold and courageous to walk in faith and follow the directives He gives you. Trust me, it may solve a much bigger issue than you think.

Notes For the Day:

-John 16:13 But when he, the Spirit of truth, comes, he will guide you into all the truth. He will not speak on his own; he will speak only what he hears, and he will tell you what is yet to come.

-Isaiah 11:3 And He will delight in the fear of the LORD, And He will not judge by what His eyes see, Nor make a decision by what His ears hear;

-Psalm 119:66 Teach me good discernment and knowledge, For I believe in Your commandments.

Homework:

Today while you are teaching, plan a moment to sit for at least 3 minutes and observe your students while they are working independently. As you are sitting ask the Holy Spirit to highlight any student that you need to monitor differently today.

_____

_____

_____

_____

_____

_____

LESSON TWENTY-FIVE

REFLECTION

In one of the districts I taught in, my students would take district assessments every three weeks. Wow! That's a lot right? The intention of this practice was to gauge where students stood academically with the hope that intervention would take place before it became an issue of academic endangerment. Whether I agreed or not, I had to administer these tests to my students.

Reflection is a good practice. It allows one to adjust accordingly in order to align with the objectives and goals that have been established. It also provides an opportunity to celebrate progress and encourage the spirit when backward movement is evident. I believe the frequency of reflection should be determined by the specific environment. Perhaps you may not want to reflect in short-term increments if you don't have a support system that will buttress and cheer you on when you fall into slumps. Shame and condemnation may be the result, depending on the particular environment. That is certainly not the mental space Our Heavenly Father desires for you.

Me being the ultra-enthusiastic, yet stern teacher that I was, I would always make a huge celebration out of reflection time. I understand that children are just that: kids! You steal the joy of learning when you make everything a competition while applying great pressure. Instead, I use to make it a celebration of how much each child's brain grew in comparison to their last assessment. Oh, it was a BIG deal! We would cheer for everyone, even if they only improved by one point. If a child rescinded, we'd still cheer them on by saying what an incredible opportunity was available for them to do even better next time. Perspective is everything!

As you reflect on your teaching practice, keep in mind that Your Heavenly Father is not a condemner. He is the lifter of your head, your bestower of grace and mercy, the collector of every single one of your tears, your strong tower, and the ultimate lover of your soul! While you are doing the best you can, celebrate the small victories. Praise your student who actually raises her hand instead of blurting out! That's a HUGE deal! Zechariah 4:10 says, "Do not despise these small beginnings, for the Lord rejoices to see the work begin, to see the plumb line in Zerubbabel's hand."

Yes, it may be true that you have a long way to get your students where you would like them to be, but you have to take it in strides. You know as well as I that overnight success is 99.9% NOT the case when you are working with students, and that is perfectly normal. Kids need time to develop into the best versions of themselves at their current age, and most times that's an incremental process. In Mark 4:28 we see even grain goes through a sequential process in order to manifest. "All by itself the soil produces grain-first the stalk, then the head, then the full kernel in the head."

Make sure you reflect, as it is your responsibility to partner to manifest growth. However, reflect in a way that honors Your Heavenly Father's Spirit as it concerns you. John 3:17 says, "For God did not send his Son into the world to condemn the world, but to save the world through him."

Notes For the Day:

-Psalm 3:3 But you, LORD, are a shield around me, my glory, the One who lifts my head high.

-Proverbs 27:19 As water reflects the face, so one's life reflects the heart.

-Hebrews 12:1 Therefore, since we are surrounded by such a great cloud of witnesses, let us throw off everything that hinders and the sin that so easily entangles. And let us run with perseverance the race marked out for us.

Homework:

Revisit one of the goals you had for yourself or your students this semester. Write down one way in which you making awesome progress towards your goal. Write down one way you can adjust what you are doing starting tomorrow to do a better job reaching this goal.

_____

_____

_____

_____

_____

_____

_____

Week 6

LESSON TWENTY-SIX

PASSION

In my opinion, passion sets mediocre teachers apart from great educators. There's just something about a teacher who has a flame in his/her soul and is ready to set all of the students ablaze with a zest and joy for learning! Can you tell the difference? When you walk down the hallways and you see the way some kids respond to certain adults and how some students' dispositions are incredibly different with one adult versus another? It's passion!

I believe passion makes anything worthwhile. Let's take a look at Jesus who endured the cross because of His passion for us! I mean who else is going to willingly go to a cross to be slaughtered gruesomely while being tormented and bullied all the way there!?? That must be sooooommmmmee outrageous degree of passion! Hebrews 12:2 says we, "fixing our eyes on Jesus, the pioneer and perfecter of faith. For the joy set before him he endured the cross, scorning its shame, and sat down at the right hand of the throne of God."

Meditate on the unfathomable passion that your Heavenly Father had for you as He went and endured the cross. Likewise, you do the same for your students. Bring joy into your lessons! Don't just teach the states of matter. Teach the states of matter using a root beer float experiment. Don't just teach character traits. Use a Disney movie to include your students' interests and analyze the attributes of various characters at the same time.

You will be astounded when you see the difference in their engagement levels and desire to attend school. When my students did independent work in class, I didn't just assign the work. I assigned the work and allowed one of the students the opportunity to choose "work music." It's all about the passion and excitement that you bring to the classroom. Can you believe I used to hype my students up and have a cheer session over the district assessments we had to take? Yup! Why not celebrate the fact that we were about to witness their brain's growth!? Kids will follow the tone you set, so set a positive and dynamic one.

Take a particular lesson that you will be teaching one day next week and revamp it. In 2 Corinthians 5:21 we see that Jesus, "For our sake He made him to be sin who knew no sin, so that in him we might become the righteousness of God." He did all of that for our sake! Why can't you be that to your kids on a smaller scale? You can, and it doesn't have to take that much work. All you have to do is insert the love you have for your kids into your lesson. It could be as simple as working towards a fun dance "brain break" in the middle of the lesson. Trust me, it'll make a world of difference in your classroom climate.

Notes For the Day:

-*John 3:16 For God so loved the world, that he gave his only Son, that whoever believes in him should not perish but have eternal life.*

-*John 19:30 When Jesus had received the sour wine, he said, "It is finished," and he bowed his head and gave up his spirit.*

-*Mark 10:45 For even the Son of Man came not to be served but to serve, and to give his life as a ransom for many.*

Homework:

Revamp one lesson you'll be teaching next week to show passion to your kids. Now sit back and watch your classroom transform!

_____

_____

_____

_____

_____

_____

_____

_____

_____

_____

_____

_____

_____

_____

_____

LESSON TWENTY-SEVEN

INTEGRITY

I was raised to be a woman of integrity. Most of us grow up with this similar value, but along the way some decide to journey down the most convenient paths instead of facing the crossroads of those hard decisions head on. Teaching is a profession that will challenge your interpretation of demonstrating what it means to be a human being who embodies integrity.

I learned very early on that the teachers' lounge would not be my sweet spot. I'd been warned of the gossip that unfolds in that place, and I knew even if that wasn't the conversation of the lounge every day, it couldn't be a place I frequented much if I was going to maintain my position as a woman who honored the words I spoke.

My very first year of teaching, I was assigned to a testing grade. The local media made it known that there were individuals who'd received harsh repercussions for being involved in student cheating scandals. I knew if I wanted to maintain my position as a stand-up woman, I couldn't allow the pressure of administration, the district, or the state department to compromise my morals and values of honesty.

One of my most poignant memories of allowing integrity to roar within me was whenever I received students who had special needs. Any teacher can sit in the room with a 504 or IEP in their files and pretend to implement a thorough plan that meets the needs of your most vulnerable learners, but I just could not do that. To call me an advocate for my students was a pleasantry. I was set ablaze for my learners each and every day! I treated them like my own children even when they were four years beyond physically being in my classroom.

You can only imagine my passion when I entered one such meeting to advocate for a child I believed had been set up to fail in the education system. I had so many questions about why this student was passed on for so long, why no one intervened, and most importantly what we could set up in the present moment to course correct and guarantee some levels of success for this student for the years to come.

My intensity was met with rote public relations commentary and injustice was all I heard reverberating between the walls of my ears. I couldn't take it, and I burst into tears! I wondered how Our Father was viewing me at this moment as I was doing my best to fulfill what He directed in Proverbs 31:8, "Speak up for those who cannot speak for themselves, for the rights of all who are destitute."

You see, Jesus never stopped speaking up for us when we were ignorantly swimming in our sins. He didn't even stop pursuing us when we were knowingly flirting with our trespasses. He held His ground in love for us and continued to stand because He knew the vision His Father had given Him.

I knew in those moments when I was fighting for my student that I had to simply do that. Fight! I couldn't back down because I knew the vision my Father had given me as a teacher. Proverbs 3:27-28 reminds us, "Do not withhold good from those who deserve it, when it is in your power to act. Do not say to your neighbor, "Come back later; I'll give it tomorrow" – when you now have it with you." As an adult, I had the ability to rise up against the politics that sat so comfortably in the room that day. It was in my power to speak up for the accommodations I knew this child needed and had a right to receive whether all who were present were in agreement or not. I had to do my part to ensure things shifted for the best that day. Is it not our kingdom duty?

Let me warn you. It will be uncomfortable. Going against the grain is never a pleasant experience, but it's worth it and necessary. Ask Our Father to awaken His Spirit in you, to walk with boldness in what He's called you to do and say. Drown out the opinions of others and submit yourself to what He said. Trust me, generations will be better because you held on to your integrity.

Matthew 10:19 says, "When you are arrested, don't worry about how to respond or what to say. God will give you the right words at the right time."

Notes For the Day:

-Luke 6:31 Do to others as you would have them do to you.

-Proverbs 21:3 To do what is right and just is more acceptable to the LORD than sacrifice.

-Proverbs 4:25-27 Let your eyes look straight ahead; fix your gaze directly before you. Give careful thought to the paths for your feet and be steadfast in all your ways. Do not turn to the right or the left; keep your foot from evil.

Homework:

Is there a scenario that took place on campus where you feel you didn't take the high road of integrity? Write down how you would have liked that scenario to unfold. If it is in your ability to change the part you played, go correct it.

LESSON TWENTY-EIGHT

REVOLUTION

There is a fine line between rebellion and revolution. Rebellion involves violent and open opposition to established authority. Whereas revolution involves a complete change in one's thinking that occasionally takes the form of resistance. This ultimately leads to a favorable fundamental change encompassing large-scale benefits for all involved. While people who are seen as rebels don't necessarily gain that name from positive associations, those who are deemed revolutionaries have changed the course of history for the better.

Throughout my teaching tenure, I was often seen as the revolutionary. How do I know this? Could it have been the way meetings somehow always included an aspect of me being cornered with, "Ms. Askew do you have anything to add?" How about my coworkers coming into my room asking my background and why I stand my ground on certain issues? Or could it have been the internal battle I would fight during every meeting trying to tell myself to keep my hands down and my mouth closed? Ha!

It wasn't long before I began to embrace this "revolutionary" side of my personality. Please don't misunderstand me. I didn't intentionally go to work looking to "pick a fight" or "ruffle anyone's feathers." I entered that school building each day with my Heavenly Father's mission on my heart: love your kids, develop and support them, then teach them. Anything that hindered that mission had to be discarded. Whenever I went to a meeting and saw that my students would suffer at the hand of politics, or the aforementioned mission would be compromised, I spoke up about it in the spirit of justice.

Jesus said in Matthew 10:34-37: "Do not suppose that I have come to bring peace to the earth. I did not come to bring peace, but a sword. For I have come to turn a man against his father, a daughter against her mother, a daughter-in-law against her mother-in-law— a man's enemies will be the members of his own household. Anyone who loves their father or mother more than me is not worthy of me; anyone who loves their son or daughter more than me is not worthy of me."

Now was Jesus saying He came to be a rebel and unleash violence on the Earth? Not even! He was saying He came to bring truth and justice to the Earth. If that meant some people who formerly associated, began to part ways because they were on opposing sides of the truth, then so be it. Regardless, He was committed to bringing the truth to all mankind as directed by His Father. The "Good News" was the favorable change that He knew would revolutionize the world order as it existed. Jesus knew the opinions of people could not supersede the cost of discipleship. He knew His mission had the potential to bring division. Nonetheless, His mission had to be accomplished.

If and whenever you find yourself in a discussion that entices you to abandon the very reason you were placed in the classroom: the advocacy of your students, don't be afraid to be bold and speak up for them. Do so respectfully of course, but do it nonetheless. More than likely, many will not always agree with you, but in a world full of leaning towers and vacillating opinions, you must be the monument that remains erect.

Just like Esther was brought to the Kingdom for the moment of saving the Jews, perhaps you were brought to your school campus for such a time as this. Did it ever cross your mind that He placed specific kids in your classroom that He wanted you to champion and discipline in love because no one else will? Did you ever think that the ideas you have were dropped in your spirit from Him because He needed a vessel to deliver them to your school campus?

If you constantly feel the revolution boiling within you, ask Him to clarify how He wants you to navigate what you are feeling? Ask Him if there is something specific He wants you to mention to your administration. Is there a certain role He desires for you to take on so that His glory may be shown through you?

Oftentimes those things that annoy you the most, the repetitive naggings you have, are bigger than just you. They are calling you into the deep to walk in the very arena that will cause others to observe you and know that you walk alongside the Mighty One. They will know that you are not on that campus by happenstance, but your steps are truly ordered by the Lord.

Notes For the Day:

-Esther 4:14 For if you remain silent at this time, relief and deliverance for the Jews will arise from another place, but you and your father's family will perish. And who knows but that you have come to your royal position for such a time as this?"

-Philemon 1:8 For this reason, although I have great boldness in Christ to command you to do what is right.

-Joshua 1:9 I've commanded you, haven't I? "Be strong and courageous. Don't be fearful or discouraged, because the Lord your God is with you wherever you go."

Homework:

In what area have you compromised the central focus of your students when you would have preferred to speak up for them? Write out what you would have said instead. Pray and ask Our Father for a "redemptive moment."

_____

_____

_____

_____

_____

_____

_____

_____

_____

_____

_____

_____

_____

_____

LESSON TWENTY-NINE

HARVESTING

Is it me or am I the only one who waits earnestly with eyes wide open, grinning from ear to ear for the moment I can see the harvest Our Father will bring forth from my sowing throughout the school year? Don't get me wrong, sowing time is equally important if not more so than harvesting, but there's this magnetism around the harvest that kickstarts your heart like a defibrillator.

Who doesn't want to know what their hard work translates into? You've been showing up every day at work, you've stayed after school to tutor, and you've even delivered instruction during Saturday school! You revamped and remixed the same lesson 15 times just to target each tier learner better with every new execution. You've prayed over the growth of your students in the face of contradictory evidence. You deserve to see all that the harvest has brought in and so do your students!

One thing I had to consistently remind myself of during the school year is the fact that I am not in charge of the harvest. In Matthew 9:38 it says, "Ask the Lord of the harvest, therefore, to send out workers into his harvest field." Did you catch that? "Ask the Lord of the harvest," which means He has sovereign control over the output that corresponds to our input.

There is no amount of work that you or I can do that will intensify this harvest. Rather we must do our best to plow the fields and sow seeds to the height of our ability. Afterwards, we rest. We allow our Father to determine the increase. Now of course, if you sow little, you will in turn reap little, but that is more about your heart posture than it is about the quantity of your input.

As you sit in glorious anticipation of your benchmark and state standardized test scores returning, do so with the knowledge that you have sown to the best of your ability. If one or several of your students doesn't grow leaps and bounds this year, trust that in Our Father's perfect timing, it will happen for that scholar. Your seeds were not planted in vain, and they will not return void just like His Word is incapable of doing. Instead, when the "Lord of the Harvest" declares it's time, the reward will be great!

On this day, whether you are sowing or preparing to receive your students' harvest, do so submitted to the truth that He is the Lord of the Harvest. Trust the unfolding of His plans. Celebrate the small victories. Celebrate the victories that you have yet to see. Rejoice in the harvest!

Notes For the Day:

-Genesis 8:22 While the earth remains, seedtime and harvest, And cold and heat, And summer and winter, And day and night shall not cease.

-2 Corinthians 9:10 Now He who supplies seed to the sower and bread for food will supply and multiply your seed for sowing and increase the harvest of your righteousness

-Luke 10:2 He told them, "The harvest is plentiful, but the workers are few. Ask the Lord of the harvest, therefore, to send out workers into his harvest field."

Homework:

Take a moment to meditate on Matthew 9:38. Declare this scripture over your life until you feel a covering of peace come over your heart.

_____

_____

_____

_____

_____

_____

_____

_____

_____

_____

_____

_____

LESSON THIRTY

VICTORY

In your opinion, does victory have a specific look or arouse a specific feeling? Is victory defined the same for everyone? How do you know that you have arrived at victory? These are all questions I've contemplated periodically while teaching. If you aren't careful, you'll allow the state department of education, your school district, and even the world to project on you this "one size fits all" template of victory. Don't worry, I'm here to encourage your heart.

Victory looks different on everyone. Take Jesus' Earthly life as an example. Jesus was victorious in myriad ways, but they all appeared distinctly different. Sometimes victory looked like Jesus simply agreeing to permit someone that was "lower" in status to baptize Him. Other times victory looked like him arriving "late" to heal someone's brother. While other times triumph looked like Him "losing" His life in the most degrading way for people who could care less about who He was or what He came to do. Wow! Talk about levels to success!

Would you say victory looks like being birthed as the Savior of the world and then deciding at the age of 12 to go missing for three days? Uhhh…I think not. However, this was what God deemed winning for Jesus at that moment. Jesus was walking in alignment with the plan that was drafted for Him when God designed our redemption story.

So let's take a look at what's going on in your life and classroom? Have you set an unjust standard of victory for all of your students? Or, have you considered where they currently are and created a wall for them to scale?

Two students immediately come to my mind: Michelle and Emilio. Emilio was a natural at academics. Learning came fairly easy to him and he excelled almost effortlessly at everything. Michelle, on the other hand, was a sweet girl who came to me with a horrid history of being sexually abused. She was a very silly little girl who enjoyed sharing stickers and wearing huge frilly bows to school. She was the ultimate girly girl. Yet Michelle would have moments where she would mentally check out of school. In those moments you could tell she'd come face to face with the trauma she endured in her vicious past.

My notion of "victory" for Emilio was different than that of Michelle's because they were each facing their own personal battles and learning to navigate the environments they'd been given in respect to their unique personalities. Victory for Michelle meant she had more moments where she was present in class vs. drifting off to be tortured by her past. Victory for Emilio showed up in the form of me pushing him past what was already academically feasible for him, although he was still in the same grade as his peers.

Take some time and reflect on this today. If Jesus' victories didn't necessarily look like what everyone else thought they should look like, what do your victories truly look like? Have you bypassed your victories or your students' victories at the infringement of other peoples' opinions? Romans 8:31 reiterates the fact that we should be more focused on what Our Father believes about us versus the speculations of human beings. It says, "What, then, shall we say in response to these things? If God is for us, who can be against us?"

Today take a moment and really ask your Heavenly Father what victory looks like for you in the context of teaching. What does victory look like for each of your students? No, you aren't watering down your standards. Instead, you are honoring each child for who and where they are, and setting milestones that will allow them to touch victory in a customized way. Dare to go against the grain of society's cookie cutter victory standard. Consult your Father's truth instead.

Notes For the Day:

-*Proverbs 21:31 The horse is made ready for the day of battle, but victory rests with the LORD.*

-*Proverbs 29:25 It is dangerous to be concerned with what others think of you, but if you trust the Lord, you are safe.*

-*Galatians 1:10 Am I saying this now to win the approval of people or God? Am I trying to please people? If I were still trying to please people, I would not be Christ's servant.*

Homework:

What does victory look like in one area of your personal life? (finances, family, marriage, friendships, mental health, ect.)

_____

_____

_____

_____

_____

_____

_____

_____

_____

_____

_____

_____

_____

_____

_____

_____

_____

_____

_____

_____

_____

Bonus

LESSON THIRTY-ONE

LOVE

One of my most memorable birthdays landed on a school day! On this day I was reminded that love is so much more than a word. Journey with me back to my 30th birthday. Yes, I went to work on my milestone birthday, and I'm so glad I did!

The weekend prior, I decided to spoil myself with a purchase in celebration of another year of life! I was a pretty fashionable teacher, always loving putting together fabulous outfits that conveyed my exuberance for being alive each day. I could always be spotted strutting across the campus in my 3.5 inch heels or gracing the imaginary catwalk in my head. Ha! If you have to show up, you might as well show up in style. It just makes your day feel so much better! Or was that all in my head? At any rate, it wasn't a stretch when I decided to purchase a special dress to wear to work on my birthday. I saw it as a little gift to myself.

Honestly, I wasn't expecting anyone to do anything special for me. I figured I'd get the usual, "Happy Birthday Ms. Askew" along with buckets of hugs as I walked down the hallway. That morning, I showed up 30 minutes before school as usual only to be greeted by a massive bulletin on my door that read "Happy Birthday Ms. Askew! We love you!" It was fabulously decorated! What a surprise! Already my day was off to an incredible start! I figured maybe the kids, and fellow teachers had schemed to surprise me with that vibrant poster before anyone arrived at school. Pretty clever surprise indeed!

I began to go about my morning routine, prepping everything for my students' arrival and positioning my mind and heart to tackle just what My Father had called me to do. I was greeted with warm embraces from my fellow teaching team after running a few errands in the building. Grrrrrr. Copies of course. It never fails. After all of that, I positioned myself at the door to greet my students. Everything seemed to be pretty normal, with the exception of the "Happy Birthdays!" added to my students' salutations.

That year, I had a team teacher. I noticed a few of my students walked into my team teacher's classroom after greeting me instead of walking straightaway into our room. Yet, that wasn't unusual, because sometimes they'd do that. I greeted the last student at the door as the tardy bell rang. I hadn't even noticed that my team teacher departed a few minutes earlier than normal. Perhaps all the text messages I was attempting to respond to before the bell rang distracted me.

As I entered the classroom, I was ambushed by my team teacher and all 44 of our students shouting "Happy Birthday Ms. Askew!" The back table was a volcano overflowing with lava wrapped presents. I thought, "As tough as I am on my students and as much as I try to show them I care about them deeply, it took nothing for them to interpret my daily interactions with them as love." They responded with such an outpouring of fondness that I'll never forget! The gifts were so thoughtful and tailored just for me! They even had more surprises planned throughout the day!

I couldn't help but to think of how Our Father lavishes His love upon us on normal days, but even more so on special days. To assume I went to work that day, thinking, at least I get to wear my special birthday dress, believing that was the end of the story. My, my did He have something else planned for me through the vessels of my team teacher and my students!

Love is an action word. It's one thing for my students to tell me they love me or even for me to tell them. However, when they express their affections towards me in hugs, gifts, showers of beautiful words, and posters, it's that much more tangible and heartfelt. Our Father went to the cross to display His greatest love for us. How much more actionable can you get than that!? If you never thought you were loved before, let this be the confirmation that you are loved beyond belief!

When you gaze around your classroom today, observe the "love." More specifically, look at the actions your students are exhibiting that say, " I love you _____ (insert your name here). Observe your actions towards them. Are you conveying a message of love and appreciation towards them or a message of frustration and annoyance? Choose carefully because your kids understand full well that love expresses itself in action.

Notes For the Day:

-1 John 3:16-18 This is how we know what love is: Jesus Christ laid down his life for us. And we ought to lay down our lives for our brothers and sisters. If anyone has material possessions and sees a brother or sister in need but has no pity on them, how can the love of

God be in that person? Dear children, let us not love with words or speech but with actions and in truth.

-1 Corinthians 13:4-8 Love is patient, love is kind. It does not envy, it does not boast, it is not proud. It does not dishonor others, it is not self-seeking, it is not easily angered, it keeps no record of wrongs. Love does not delight in evil but rejoices with the truth. It always protects, always trusts, always hopes, always perseveres. Love never fails.

-1 Corinthians 13:1-3 If I speak in the tongues of men or of angels, but do not have love, I am only a resounding gong or a clanging cymbal. If I have the gift of prophecy and can fathom all mysteries and all knowledge, and if I have a faith that can move mountains, but do not have love, I am nothing. If I give all I possess to the poor and give over my body to hardship that I may boast, but do not have love, I gain nothing.

Homework:

Write down one way you can show the action of love to your own family today and to your students as well.

_____

_____

_____

_____

_____

_____

_____

_____

_____

T E A C H Supernaturally

My Notes

T E A C H Supernaturally

For More Resources

@livingin_hd

https://www.livinginhd.org

Made in the USA
San Bernardino, CA
16 December 2018